Manifest Dreams Into Reality
How to manifest your positive goals and dreams into reality.

by
Celest Klatt

Dedication

This book is dedicated to my husband Steve Klatt, my deceased beloved mother Eleanor Miller, my deceased beloved collie Felisa, my cat Trixie, my father Robert C. Miller; my hairdresser Mindy Metzgar.

For all their love and support. I honor them and want to thank them from the bottom of my heart. God continue to Bless them.

About the author: CELEST KLATT is a psychic-clairvoyant. Celest uses her gift as a healer and medium. She also performs Reiki, past life regressions, and hypnosis. She has worked hands on with many police agencies throughout the northeast, as well as with respected doctors and hospitals around the world.

Celest works live through Internet readings and is one of the top world known psychic-clairvoyants in the field. Her clients are some of the most respected people in the country. Her clientele consists of people from all lifestyles. They include ordinary men and women, actors, physicians, law enforcement personnel and veterinarians. Local pet stores and veterinary offices needing to diagnose illness in cats and dogs have even called upon her.

She is a third generation Psychic Clairvoyant. Both her great grandmother and mother were very gifted clairvoyants, and mediums.

Celest has been reading for 38 years, she works seven days a week and it is rare she turns anyone down who needs a reading. She thinks of her clients well-being first. Her clients always come first. Celest is highly recommend by the medical field because of her being exceptional at finding health problems. She is highly respected, loves animals and takes in all the sick ones to love and nuture them. Celest has had her rough times mostly in the middle of her life. Unfortuntely, she was in a very abusive relationship 10 years ago. A psychic cannot read their own life, this is normal. They need to learn and get to their outcome just like everyone else. She recently got married in November 2004 to a wonderful man who is clairvoyant and does professional astrology charts. Celest is very spiritual and spends a lot of time talking with Angels, God, and her spirit guide George. Celest has no children, but adores them. She says children and animals are such pure souls sent to us. Most importantly, what Celest teaches, and what you will learn in this book, is you can always change your life around for the better and manifest your dreams into reality.

TABLE OF CONTENTS

1

LET ME HELP SHOW YOU THE WAY

The goal of this book is to help people gain the simple tools they need to get to where they want, and need to be in life. Trust me; it is very simple and very effective if you practice it. Too often, I see people manifesting negative aspects into their lives, but wanting positive aspects. With this book, I want to show people how they can reverse, and eliminate the negative forces that surround them, or to better your life in any direction. Once the reader has done that, he or she is ready to accentuate the positive. I want you, the reader, to know that you can be successful in love, finance, friendship, and health. With the tools that I give you, you too can be successful at accomplishing your life's goals.

The reason I say I can do this is that I am a genuine Psychic Clairvoyant. I have two spirit guides that have assisted me throughout my life. My primary guide is named George. I first started seeing him when I was four years old. At first, he came to me as a white hazy figure. He did this so as not to scare me when I was young. By the time I turned eight he began to show himself in his true form as a man.

To me, he is like any other man to look at; he is without any strange or noticeable differences. He stands about six foot two, thin, and has silver flowing hair, which he always pulls back in a ponytail and goes three inches past his shoulders. He parts his hair in the middle, and he always appears very neat and clean cut. Going by his looks, his apparent age is in his mid-fifties. Depending on the time of day his attire changes. Normally he is dressed casually in blue jeans and a loose fitting shirt. When it gets to be the end of the day, he will show up in a smoking jacket. This is his way of telling me that I am done for the day. Also, if he feels I need to rest or recharge he will do so. One more thing about his appearance; he has piercing blue eyes, and dimples.

Now, George will speak or contact me through various means. How he does communicate is not in any particular order of importance. The form of communication is the one that he thinks is used best for each individual situation. He communicates with me through Clairaudient, which is through hearing, Clairsentient, which is through feelings or "Empathic", and he also uses Clairessence, which is like scent or smell. No matter the form he chooses, it is all done through channeling. Over the years I have learned to know George more and more, and you can say we have got the system down. We connect smoothly and very clear.

The other spirit guide I have is a small Persian girl named Sherma. She appears to be about twelve years old.

She has long, shimmering black hair and almond eyes. Do not be confused. The age they appear is not their true age, as they are 30 years old on the otherside as all others who crossed over are 30. The reason they appear looking a certain age is they crossed over at their one or two lifetimes on earth at that age. That is their way of showing us what age they crossed over. As when I do medium work, the client receiving the messages from their deceased loved ones can identify them quickly if they come at the age they crossed over to the otherside. If they came to me looking 30 like we all are on the otherside, it would confuse the client or loved ones. Sherma is not my primary spirit guide; however, she does give me more of the nurturing aspects in regards to the feelings and pain the client is going through.

We can have more than one spirit guide, however one is always the primary spirit guide. They are all assigned to us for different purposes. We do not have tons of spirit guides, usually only between two or three. It is important to realize that each one is important for its own particular reason. However, whenever I do readings it always comes through George.

When I first saw George, I remember being scared out of my wits; I went running to my mother and she soothed my fears. At the time, my mother was a very gifted psychic, but she never really explained to me that this could happen to me... this gift I was born with. I guess she stalled too long and I found out myself. I first realized something was different about me when I was around seven years old. When I turned seven, I would blurt things out in school and they would happen. As a young psychic, you tend to blurt things out fast, almost in an uncontrollable manner. It just comes out before you think about it. I have a vivid memory of telling one of my classmates in school that her mother was going to pass away and the next day she was not in school because her mother had crossed over.

I did not know any better at that age. I should of said it in a warning matter, instead of blurting it out so harsh. However, as I said, when you are young you blurt it out without thinking. I was not accepted for awhile in school, but others got use to me very quickly and wanted me to read them. It is important to know that if I am told by George my Spirit Guide, that someone is going to cross, I am suppose to give the information to my client. I have a gift and you never withhold from someone or lie who you are giving a reading to. I try to let them know that it would be a good time to tell their loved ones how much they love them and to clear their conscious or unfinished business before their loved ones cross to the otherside. I always try to tell them to put their affairs in order, and for them to forgive others and to forgive themselves. Do the unfinished business, whatever it may be. The readings I do now are always one on one, or with only those that the client wants present. I am a very blunt Psychic and will never tell anyone something they just want to hear. I speak the truth. I would never tell others about a specific client's reading. I am extremely confidential. In fact, I use many examples in this book concerning what I suggest has helped my clients; yet all names have been changed and any obvious trademarks about them have been removed to protect their privacy.

Lying in bed as a small child, I would see those who had crossed over almost every night. My mother's house was always filled with police officers on their lunch break as my family was, and still is, in law enforcement. I would tell the officers what their day was going to be like, and who committed the crimes they were investigating. That was how I won their trust and began working with the police.

I am extremely accurate in matters of health. While working as a nurse, and an EMT, jobs I had for many years, I would know when patients were about to cross over. I remember working the night shift, which is a time when many patients pass away. I would get the tags ready before they passed and a few hours later, I would be tagging the bodies at the morgue. I also was able to see what was wrong with them and would get so frustrated when the doctors did not prescribe the proper treatment or medication. My hands were tied and that was very sad. Repeatedly, I would voice my opinions to them and eventually they began to trust my abilities. I gave up nursing after a few years as it was frustrating seeing what could and could not be done. Also, I found that the deaths of others can be very draining on me personally. Because I could feel what the family members were going through, physically and emotionally. As a psychic you need to cleanse yourself from everyone you read. It can be very draining because you are picking up how a client feels regarding illness or emotions. I can also get into someone's mind as an empath, and see what they are thinking or the person the client is asking of. This is similar to a health reading. I am not a mind reader. However, I specialize in health issues and enjoy helping to find health matters when the medical field professionals fail. No matter how far or near, I will give them my help.

I have helped many people with all the facets of their lives including:

Relationship problems.
Health concerns.
Legal troubles.
Career decisions.
Loved ones and relatives that have passed on.
Animal readings and also matters of their health and

mental well-being.

Medium Work

My readings are very quick because I am getting answers very fast from George. I am also an empathic healer. This means I can feel what is wrong with others, health, emotions and also get into their minds as an empath and help solve my clients' emotional worries, or put them back on the right path. I have often been called upon to get into someone's head to see what is causing their emotional and/or health problems. Again, I am not a mind reader, but I am an empath who can feel what is going on in a person's mind. I am living what they are thinking at the time I am in their head. This helps a lot in the medical profession.

Always think positive, as negative thoughts bring negative energy. Please also remember that there is no such thing as a spell. I have been asked a countless number of times if someone has placed a spell over a client and I always tell them, NO! "Spells" are nothing more than excess negative energy placed on the recipient without their knowledge. If you do a simple negative cleansing, it will counteract the negative energy. Or, follow this book and you will not pick or cling onto the negative energy. So do not pay anyone to rid a spell, they are only taking your money. There is no such a thing as a spell. I will go into more detail concerning cleansings later in this book, so do not worry if you think someone is sending negative energy at you. You can defeat it and be able to manifest the positive once again without any real problem.

When I do a reading, I use my Psychic Clairvoyant gift that I talked a little about earlier. As an empath, I can feel what others are feeling. An example of this is; if I were reading someone who has a headache, I would feel it. Therefore, I need to cleanse myself properly after each reading so that I can free myself of the energies of my clients. When I am tuned into a client during a reading, I see the past, present or future. I am living and seeing what they are living and seeing. When I do that, it can take a toll on me emotionally. I often find myself living their lives out as an empath and so I feel the stress and emotions that go along with it. Over the years, I have learned to build up my tolerance to other people's emotions and stresses. For that reason, I have an extremely high clientele list. So, once again, I always cleanse myself before I move on to the next client. It is this cleansing process I will be sharing with you later in the book, so you can become more attuned to your own positive energy.

I am not always doing readings, and I try not to walk around all day reading people. First, I do not think it would be the right thing to do. In addition, I feel the reading would not be what I would want it to be. I am always rested up and in a good state of mind during all my readings. I also stay very spiritual and very close to God. I pray a great deal and keep thinking positive thoughts. There have even been times when I have done a reading on woman that is pregnant and they do not even know it yet. In one such situation, I found myself coming down with morning sickness as soon as I began reading the client... even before she knew she was pregnant. I always tell my clients I am not a doctor and I am not diagnosising an illness. However, I always give them the information I receive regarding their health so that they can take the information to a doctor and take the proper steps.

To me it is all worth it. All the good I have done over the years helping loved ones make peace with their family and friends that have crossed over, the medical problems I have helped diagnose, and connecting clients to their kindermates, remind me of why I do it. I have loved and cherished each client I have helped over the years. I hope with this book I will be able to help more.

2

FROM THAT LIFE TO THIS

The Otherside

Everyone around us in this life has known us at one point in our past lives; your neighbors, co-workers, my clients who I have read over the years are all from my past lives. We are usually reincarnated with others who have been in a past life before and are usually a few blocks from where we are living currently. In fact, I would say that even the person that helped me to publish this book is someone I have known in a past life.

It is true that almost everyone has lived numerous lifetimes. For many this can be almost one hundred, while for others it can be as few as sixty. What this means is that when we move from place to place, moving away from our relatives and friends, in fact what is happening is that we are moving towards a former loved one from another lifetime or another past life. No matter where we move to, there is always someone from one of our past lives. It is a constant circle of carnations that surrounds us all the time.

I will share with you an example of how this works: My neighbor is living near me but moving to a different country in the near future. When he and his family move, they will be moving near those that they have known at some point in their past lives. However, the people that will be moving in their place will be someone that has known me in a past life. When you consider all the people you have met over the years, in this lifetime as well as all the relatives you have, which includes cousins, aunts, uncles, co-workers, mates, wives, husbands, siblings, and acquaintances, you will then have an idea of how many people your soul has met in it's travels.

This keeps a stable circle of souls reconnecting from many of our lifetimes on earth. This may help you understand why we can geographically move around and still be in a circle of people from our past lives.

When we have passed on from this lifetime on earth, our souls are cleansed. However, in certain circumstances those who are evil are not automatically cleansed. Some roam like zombies in a room until they take God into their heart, while some are forced to carnate immediately after crossing. They do not even have a chance to read their records, past contract, or reunite with loved ones. They are very dark. At the same time, everything that we have completed is recorded, so that when we are on the otherside we can review our past lives. Even during the night, our souls in this lifetime travel to the otherside to check out the contract we wrote to see if it is on track with what is happening. Remember, our minds are separate from our soul. The soul wrote the contract and is saying to the mind, come on lets make a move on this. The soul is in the center of our chest between the breast. As clean souls on the otherside, we then decide what we need to work on in our next lives when we are reincarnated back to this world. After we cross over to the otherside, we do not feel pain or sadness like we do here...no bad emotions, just pure happiness and no jealousy. Those on the otherside can see what we are doing, and know it will be ok that no matter what, it will all work out. There are no worries on the otherside. If a soul on the otherside has a kindermate, mother, dad....and they are still alive, it only seems like one month to our 30 years until they see us. So, if someone lives 30 years longer after a loved one crosses, to the loved one who crossed to the otherside, time is differential until they reunite with their loved one. There is no hurry, unless you are a dark entity or choose to reincarnate quickly.

Many times an infant will pass away and they can reincarnate over to the same mother they had originally, if she gets pregnant again within a few months, usually 6-9 months. This can occur especially if the mother had some circumstances where she became ill and the infant was affected. The soul is then offered a chance to come back if she gets pregnant again within nine months. The infant soul is then reincarnated back into the mother and is offered a healthy body.

When we cross to the otherside, it is a wonderful place. Yes, you can eat if you wish, but of course you will not gain weight, good thing!! I have astro traveled there and it is a soft rosy color, when evening is near, with a warm comfortable temperature. They have many meetings and get togethers on the otherside, almost like a reception. There is a large room filled of loved ones and souls reconnecting. Clients always ask me, "Celest why would we ever come back to this hard, sometimes cruel world if we are surrounded by beauty and love?"

We think this now, but when we are on the otherside we do not sit around saying things like; "Geeze, I don't want to go back and go through a bad marriage again," or "That's just what I need, another life where I have acne and can't get a date for the prom." On the otherside we do not feel that pain we experienced. We just want to come back over and do it again and do it correctly. We are never forced to come back, and to some that may seem hard to believe. For most souls, it is a choice that is made when they decide to do so; except like I mentioned, evil souls have no choice, and we do choose to come back to be perfected

What A Pure Soul Is

A pure soul feels no pain, and it does not feel hate, jealously, anger or even frustration. In fact, the real goal of a soul is to attain perfection. When a person is born, their soul is pure. We are all given a fresh start. Still, we can carry on soul cell memories to the next lifetime. It is only through the life that is lived on this earth that it becomes tainted. For some people, the lives they have lived become so tainted that they are considered evil. But, they made that choice. It was not charted on their contract, please understand that. On the other hand, someone can be mentally ill...maybe a chemical imbalance, but knows right from wrong. This is a different case and they need to come back and do it again since they knew what they were doing, verses someone who has a chemical imbalance and does not know the difference between right and wrong.

There are a few things that can break up this cycle of reincarnation where the soul chooses to continue onto this world, once we get to the otherside. The first is if in this life we are incredibly evil. This does not mean someone that cheated on their wife or cursed often. This is just the middle learning. I am talking about murderers, serial rapists, terrorists and so on, as well as those that do not care or see they have done terrible things. If this is the life that is lived on this earth, then as soon as this type of person crosses, their souls are immediately cleansed and sent back to repeat their lifetime on earth to see if they can get it right. Their soul is pure and they are placed into someone who is pregnant and they will have to do it all over again as a clean pure soul. It is important to realize, we all have a pure soul when we are reincarnated over to this side, and people like Bin Laden or Jeffrey Dahmer, that kill and eat body parts have no choice but to reincarnate immediately as soon as they are pulled over to the otherside.

The second way is in situations like someone who in their lives has refused to accept God into their hearts; and have done terrible things but not to the degree of the above I just mentioned. They are put into a room and they just sort of roam with others until they accept God. In time, their Spirit Guides come and bring them to the good level on the otherside and take them out of this room.

The last way is the way all souls eventually want to end after leaving this lifetime on earth. This means you have lived a good life, and accepted God into your heart. Your soul is fulfilled when you have struggled valiantly, made it through the bumps in the road and passed, just like taking a test. You have done everything that you felt was the right thing to do. You worked on it and did not give up and you did everything in your power to remain positive. The keys to that definition are the words; valiant and integrity. The following are the meanings of these two words:

Valiant: Marked by, exhibiting, or carried out with courage persistence or determination.

Integrity: Adherence to a code of sincerity, honesty and candor; the avoidance of deception, artificiality, or shallowness.

Therefore, to get it right in this lifetime, a person should try to be; good, (valiant, and with integrity,) keep God in your heart and remain positive. Treat others well and also do not forget about the animals. I cannot force or make you do any of these things. What I can do is let you know what is expected and give you the ways that you can make doing these things easier. For many years, I have been giving readings to clients to help them with their troubles. With the help of my Spirit Guide George, I have been able to help others help themselves. I am here to guide you through the middle of your journey.

Your Contract

As I mentioned before, after we cross over to the otherside, we do not feel pain or sadness like we do here. There are no bad emotions, just pure happiness. There is no hurry to return unless you are a dark entity or choose to reincarnate back over fast.

Generally when we cross over to the otherside, everyone, other than evil, is given the choice as to whether we want to be reincarnated. After we cross and we have decided to come back to earth, we write out a contract. There is a beginning and an end to each contract. The middle of the contract is the part that we live out and contains the steps that we work on to get to the end. The middle is very in-depth and we can change it as it comes and goes…with both the good times and the bad. My clients struggle with time frames. It is very difficult to wait for things to happen. Most of us are all impatient. As we prepare our contract, we review our past lives in the hall of records. We are given the choice of being reincarnated to within approximately 60 miles around those we have loved in our previous life. This includes neighbors, co-workers, and bosses, even some of the people reading this book. This also includes those that have helped me in writing this book and getting it out to you. This is known as the Circle of Carnation.

Although we have the same soul, carnation after carnation after carnation, we always start fresh. In regards to a spirit guide, they have at least one or two, and very seldom, four to five lifetimes on earth. They happened to learn the middle of their contract (the free will aspect) much faster than what they were expected to accomplish. That is why they are asked to be a Spirit Guide. Most Spirit Guides go through a rough hard lesson in their few lifetimes on earth. They are highly respected.

Many clients have asked me, "Celest why would God make a baby be miscarried or die from an abortion?" The truth is, God does not do anything like that. God never places a soul in a baby that is going to be leaving the world before its birth.

I have also been asked, "Celest why does someone choose to die when they are still an infant or a day after their birth?" or "Why would they choose to suffer painfully with leukemia or some other disease for their short lives?" First, it should be known that these are pure souls. A pure soul is one of a child or an animal. We are all reincarnated clean, and our souls begin to commence with a fresh start. What we do from there is our own lesson. Do not get me wrong, you can be 88 and have a pure soul because you were a good person your entire life. Speaking of your cell makeup, a pure soul is at the purest when you are younger as a child. They did not have much time to imperfect it like an older person.

Those souls who have written in their contract to come

back for a very short lifetime have their reasons. For example, they might want to find a cure regarding the illness they had endured in a previous short lifetime and on the other hand a life could be short due to the free will of the mother. Perhaps she is taking drugs which ultimately harms the fetus. Remember, God never plants a soul if it will be aborted. However, in this situation the mother is harming her health by taking drugs. This is her free will and she is off the path harming the fetus in the process. If the baby dies, this could be a wake up call to the mother. This does not always succeed, because as humans we still have the gift of "free will." Good or bad…free will.

Another reason is a soul may have had the same illness in a prior lifetime, and they believe that maybe a family member or someone will start to operate a fundraiser for the disease or try to become a scientist to make a cure, so they decide to recarnate to help this cause. What needs to be understood is that as souls, we still have the soul cell memories of our past lives and we have kept the wisdom of those lives.

These are examples of souls that have chosen, for one reason or another, to have a very short middle of the contract. Our souls know we have more things to learn to become the true soul we want to be.

We write in the beginning of the contract, the loved

ones we had in other lifetimes that we would like to spend time with in the next lifetime if we wish. If you had a kindermate in your last life on earth, you two would sit down and say, "Lets come back the next lifetime and see if we can get it right this time." We write in when we want to come back and the purpose of the new life we are about to choose. Then we write the end, how long we want to live and what we wish to have in the end of our lifetime. Please know that when we write the age of our preferred passing we can cut the cord sooner or stay a little longer...we can revise it some. But, also remember we need to take care of ourselves. We cannot just let ourselves go. For example, if you wrote in your contract you want to live to be 80, you still need to see a doctor and get your checkups. You have to keep taking care of yourself. The middle of the contract is the journey. The journey is how to get there, how to get what we are coming back for. We can even write in old kindermates, or mates we once had in the lifetime on earth and reincarnate back with them.

The difference between a soulmate and a kindermate is simple. Soulmates are those who are dead and are on the otherside now. If you are getting a reading from a psychic and they talk of a person being your soulmate, I would question them. A genuine psychic knows a soulmate is one who is on the otherside and has passed away. You will meet with them on the otherside when you crossover, a spouse or mate. Kindermates are alive and are in this lifetime on earth. Almost always, kindermates were with us before in a past life. We have at least four kindermates in one lifetime on Earth, but they are in different degrees. Some are at a higher level than others. However, it is possible that the second highest kindermate can be better for you than the first kindermate because of cell mind memory problems or soul cell memory. I have seen so many times someone gives up on a kindermate because they are not making any progress. Please remember, we are all learning in this journey and some learn more than others and at a faster rate of speed. Just like one kindermate is in Harvard and the other is in kindergarten. Be patient, they are still kindermates and will catch up.

All souls start off the same, yet we are all distinct and different. Again, we choose what age we want to be when we crossover. However, we do not choose the 'how' or 'where' of our deaths.

I will go over the way it works using a very hypothetical situation with a man named William. William has crossed over to the otherside and since he was not evil he can take his time deciding, when he will carnate over. He decides to wait around maybe for a loved one such as his wife in this last past life who too will eventually join him on the otherside before reincarnating. Finally, she shows up. William then decides to reincarnate shortly after. He will then go to the great hall of records where there is stored the complete history of all his past lives. He finds in the records that he has spent most of his time in one area and he rarely traveled, due to a fear of doing so. He also sees that he has always been a good parent. That being the case, he chooses not to spend too much time considering having children. As he reads more, he realizes that the last life was really hard and he wants this one to start easier but he would like a little struggle after he leaves school.

William then writes out his contract. He is not interested in having children and he would like to spend time traveling. Then he writes down that he would like to find this particular kindermate and help them to achieve a successful life in the world. He would write out, as we all do, the things we want to do to perfect ourselves. We do not write in our contract, 'I want to come back and be more handsome or dress nicer.' You do not care about that on the otherside. You only want to carnate over if you choose to learn what you failed to learn in the last lifetime. So, during all these past lives, we keep trying to perfect from the last lifetime we had on earth. We do not go backwards.

William then writes the end of his contract saying that he would like to pass on when he is 63. After the contract is written, William is given a Spirit Guide to direct him in his lifetime on earth. He is then carnated over, and his soul is planted into a mothers womb. He has been successfully born and he is a healthy baby. His mind does not know what his soul has chosen for him. Nevertheless, he sketched it out on the otherside and is now here to put it all together. This is very important when someone picks an age to cross when they are on the otherside writing their contract, if they pick the age of 60 they still can cross early if they do not take care of themselves, cut the cord, give up, or if they are murdered.

When someone is murdered, it is not that they chose to do so. The murdered individual is in fact the victim of a dark entity, or an extremely tainted soul. This happens far too much, sadly to say. Young children abducted and murdered. They did not choose this, of course, but got in the close vicinity of a dark entity. It is during the middle of our contract that we can stray off our path and go to the dark.

I would also like to take this time to share my sympathies with those that have had loved ones taken from them on 9\11. The victims of the terrorist attacks were killed by Evil. Also, I share my sympathies to the victims of Iraq, the men and woman, these good souls who are working to help others. The key is how you live the middle out so you can get to the end of the contract you wrote, to perfect and to learn. I often tell my clients that if you see a homeless man or woman, tilt your head to them or take your hat off to them. They have chosen to learn a hard lesson in their lifetime. They wanted to come back and experience the hardest lesson. They do not write down, 'I want to become homeless,' however, they choose to learn any hard lesson they are given. When we write our contracts, it is in a general sense such as, 'I want to experience as much as I can learn to better myself to the fullest degree,' or, 'I want to see if I can maintain my integrity even though I may have it easy.'

Even a person who has so many heartaches or problems, if they keep trying to pull themselves out of it and do not give in to the bad times, they are learning at a very high level. When you hit rock bottom and are doing something about it, you are learning your lesson very well and then some.

Many times, people think they are being punished when life is dealing them a hard hand. The truth is that they just happen to be hitting many snags, or they are in the hard middle times of their contract. It does not mean that they wrote a terrible contract. Nobody, not even one who will become a Spirit Guide, writes in their contract, 'I would like to reincarnate and be murdered or be in a domestic violence relationship or any bad situation.' It is how you turn it around to better it.

As I mentioned prior, Spirit Guides are those who learned in their lifetimes, beyond and above most regular people. When they pass to the otherside, they are asked to become a spirit guide. They do not have to be a spirit guide if they wish not too. Nevertheless, most of the time they do not refuse.

So it is not how they learned faster than humans, it is that they started out like us and learned quickly the same things we have and will learn. We all have that chance because we all get a fresh clean start. Do not confuse the clean start with soul cell memory problems. As I stated earlier, when you cross over, your soul is cleansed. That does not mean the soul does not remember the pain. What it does mean is that the soul no longer gives it any thought. It is when they are carnated on Earth their soul sort of has a mind of its own and can remember the hard times...the fears. This is a protection a type of warning to watch out so we do not make the same mistake. This is a soul cell memory.

If we do not heal our pain in this lifetime, our soul stores a memory of it. This memory can affect you in your next lifetime, over and over, if you do not heal it. In this book, I will show you how to manifest the good things in your life as well as how to banish the negative. To manifest the good or to banish the bad you do not need many tools, or spend a lot of money to get what you want out of life. Your mind and your soul are very powerful things and I will show you how to use them in your everyday life.

Help From The Otherside

Fortunately, we have been given help from the otherside to aid us in overcoming our troubles here on this world. There are Spirit Guides, angels, animal totems, and even our loved ones that have crossed-over. Talk aloud to your loved ones that have passed and to Angels. Always speak aloud for they cannot read our minds. They hear you and watch over us. Also, remember pets that have passed on are also being taken care of by Spirit Guides. When pets pass on, they are not reincarnated as they are pure and have no lessons to be learned.

Spirit Guides

Unlike us, spirit guides only have one or two lifetimes on earth. However, sometimes at most they may have up to four. The knowledge they accumulate is equal to over 70 lifetimes for us. Regardless, we all start out the same. They are not made Spirit Guides on their contract. They worked and earned their name.

A Spirit Guide will live their lifetime on earth and will pass with excellence. Some examples, you lose your job, or your husband or wife is leaving you. Instead of giving up or causing pain or trouble with your husband or wife, you would instead keep searching and trying to find a job. The degree of how hard you try to get what you want or to solve something plays a big part in your success. Instead of just divorcing your wife or husband, seek counseling or talk it out with them. Unless it is a question of physical or mental safety, try not to give in to the hard times. These are just examples. Some other examples include:

If a family member is very ill and maybe even bedfast, try all you can to do whatever you can to help them in their situation. You might find a homeless dog or cat that is maybe sick or nervous. Instead of having it put to sleep, give it a good home or find it one. That is how we reach the end. How we decide to complete these everyday tasks or hard times is what is placed in our record on the otherside. Do not think it is only how you deal with the bad and hard aspects of life, but also the good. If you find you have done all you had on your contract or near all, when you pass over you would then be asked to become a Spirit Guide.

Not too many are able to do so much in a few lifetimes

like a Spirit Guide has done. That is what makes them standout from the other souls. It is these souls that are asked to come back as Spirit Guides. If they agree to become a Spirit Guide they are assigned to someone and will be with this person until the day that person crosses back over to the otherside. If someone passes their lifetimes on earth in flying colors and offers to come back and spend a long lifetime on earth as a Spirit Guide, they are a special soul. They have earned it. Spirit Guides are given only one person to look after. They will be with you until the day you cross over. We all have Spirit Guides. Even the souls who turn dark have Spirit Guides. Remember this is because they had a clean soul when they carnated over, but turned dark. I personally can not imagine being a Spirit Guide to a terrorist. That is a very difficult job.

When a spirit guide is assigned to someone and that someone passes away and crosses to the otherside, the Spirit Guide assigned to that soul is no longer with them once they make it to the otherside. Now, I am told by George, my Spirit Guide, that they do speak after they are on the otherside but very little and the Spirit Guide is no longer with that soul. They have done their work. Those who were your spirit guide will be on the otherside doing work. There is so much to be done on the otherside. Not hard work, but spiritual work.

For example when someone passes suddenly, their soul feels confused, like when you get back from vacation, or move to a different house. You may not know what to do at first. Some souls just do not feel at home. So, there are Spirit Guides who are there for those who need a little more special attention after they cross. It is almost like a hospital setting. They wrap them in blankets keeping them warm and nurturing them until they are adjusted. Another example is when someone has a long-term illness. Not always, but sometimes they are so worn out even after they cross over they need some extra rest and TLC. Spirit Guides on the otherside tend to them. It makes the transaction over smooth and comforting. Even animals have Spirit Guides take them to the otherside after they pass away. They speak to them in a way so that they understand what is happening. They tend to them and foster them and you will see your pets that have crossed-over when you cross. We all will see our beloved pets.

As I mentioned, my main spirit guide is named George. He is with me most of the time, however, Spirit Guides do go to the otherside and have meetings or study. You can even talk aloud to your Spirit Guide and tell them to leave. As a psychic Clairvoyant, I have done this with George. There are times when I just do not want to have my Spirit Guide around. On the other hand, if I need to tune into

George, I call his name aloud and he comes to me.

George tells me that Spirit Guides cannot read the minds of the ones they are assigned to look over and it is always best to speak aloud.

Now, during readings George can read my thoughts, regarding the client's question and gives it back to me mentally, but that is only during a reading.

It needs to be understood that no psychic is 100 percent accurate. Only God is 100 percent accurate. George gives me the correct information using all his wisdom. Still, if I do not translate it properly, it is my mistake, not his. However there are times George is not to give out an answer, this is extremely rare but is due to the fact the client had on her contract she did not want to have help in this area, she (or he) wanted to learn on their own. Maybe it was the area she wanted to strengthen. Over time, if you have any ability to be a clairvoyant you will learn how your Spirit Guide communicates with you. Spirit Guides when you hear them, sound like a high pitch sound...a vibration. Every psychic Clairvoyant gets information different from their spirit guides; we do not get the same form or symbols of communication.

We all have spirit guides, even Osama Bin Laden, just imagine being his! We can go off path and become dark and hurt others. However, no matter what, our spirit guide is assigned to us until the day we cross over or die. It is considered a great honor to become a spirit guide. In addition, you do not have to be a guide again after you are one. On a side note if you are asked to become a spirit guide you do not have to do so, they do not draft spirit guides.

Animals

Animals do go to the otherside and stay where spirit guides are tending to them. We will all see our pets on the otherside. Many times, I have had clients ask me about their loved ones that have crossed over in relation to an animal they have seen on this side. I had an aunt crossover and a little while later I saw a puppy or a cat that had her eyes or even a certain mannerism that reminded me of her.

However, you must realize that we never carnate over as animals. The reason why your pet's eyes or personality reminds you of your loved one is that our loved ones send us pets. Those on the otherside have no problem communicating with higher forms of animals. Many times, they will see to it that we are placed in a position to choose a certain pet. At the same time, you could be out looking for a pet to own and a loved one that has crossed over may very well see a certain pet that is deserving of a good owner with your qualities so he/she will steer us together. Those who crossed will send birds or rabbits to your yard. This is their way of sending love and looking out for you. For example, when my mother crossed my dad would see a bird outside his windowsill through two harsh winters. This bird would nestle outside his window in extremely cold, snowy weather. This was a sign that my mother has sent to my dad. It is a comfort to know our loved ones are sending out to us. However, there is a difference between pets and animal totems

Animal Totems do work and they are made to protect us. We all have an animal totem. They are not spirit guides. We do not get to pick our totem of choice. We are given one that best suits us. Just like we do not pick our spirit guides. They are assigned to us. I have noticed over the years of reading it does not matter what you are like in regards to your personality; for example, if you are a tough person your totem is not necessarily a wolf. It may be a bird. There are many cases when a person sees their totem as clear as a family pet. Even the neighbors can see them hanging out near the window if it is a cat for example. My husband and I recently started seeing a cat totem in our house. I have a cat and this can drive me crazy. Not sure half the time if it is my cat Trexie or the totem.

There is a simple exercise to find what your animal

totem is; this is the same thing I have used for my clients:

1. Sit in a quiet room and keep your feet flat on the ground, while you rest your back against the back of the chair. Close your eyes and ask for the white light from the Holy Spirit to circle you and keep you safe. Always do this when in doubt of evil or fear. (I will have more on this technique later in the book.)

2. Imagine you are in a dense forest all alone; you are walking through the woods very calmly. Ask to see your animal totem; ask to have it appear in front of you. As you walk in these dense woods, you are walking slow and even stopping occasionally to make sure you do not miss it from appearing.

3. Start looking around and peek through the trees searching for your totem. It will appear to you. Keep your mind open and clear. Do not try to imagine any special kind of animal or bird to appear.

4. When you see the totem say to it – "I honor your appearance and will honor you always." Soon you will feel a bond with it as you look it in the eyes and become friends.

5. Open your eyes and feel the peace over you.

You will notice that same day or in a few days that animal or bird in magazines around you or on TV or even in a department store you may come across a statue of it.

What I highly recommend you do is buy a few, at least 2-3, statue forms of your totem, or pictures, and keep them in your house or apartment. I keep a picture and a statue of mine, a wolf on my desk in my office.

Angels

Angels do take form of human beings when they are helping someone. I have seen them with wings and have talked to an angel that looked like a young man on the street. I had a bad car accident twenty plus years ago and I would like to recount to you that very scary day.

*   *   *   *   *

It was the middle of winter in the northeast of the United States. It was dark out and I was on my way to school. It was snowing with some freezing rain early in the morning hours. As I was driving along I hit a patch of ice, and my car hit a guard rail. It spun around in a circle and ended up smashing into a steep hill. The next thing I remember is being on a large steep embankment off the road surrounded by my demolished vehicle. I remember I had nothing left to my new car but half a door on the driver's side. I was spitting glass out of my mouth when I saw a very handsome young man right next to me. The young man had light brown hair and he graciously bent down and looked in my window.

"You will be ok! Help is coming," he said very calmly and soothingly.

"Wait please! Don't leave me." I told him as he stood up straight.

I did not know who this young man was, but I did not want to be left there all alone on a steep hill in a storm. Before I knew it, after a split second he was gone. Within a few minutes, the fire department and paramedics arrived and they had a terrible time getting me on the stretcher, due to the large amounts of snow and ice. After a while, I asked them if they had seen this young man and they said, "Lady there are no footprints to be found going up or down the hill." I knew it was an angel. Moreover, nobody could have walked on that icy hill without slipping or falling. The fire department rescuers could not even stand on their own two feet, as it was so icy and snowy.

Angels are all around us and sent to us in human like form, just like you and I look. We do not realize it, but Angels are always around us in body form like you and I. Angels do not have a gender. I seem to have a bad habit myself, as I call them she or he. Angels are messengers of God. They protect and guide us. Angels are always willing to help us, but we have to call on them and accept their assistance. Angels are never a deceased relative. Here is a few things I want to give you that you can do to connect with your Angels.

1. *Talk aloud to Angels and make it simple and clear.*

2. *Visualize Angels around you, this will help open doors and you will be able to feel their presence by doing this.*

3. *Write down on paper a few things you would like Angels to know. For example, what you want or need from life. Do not make a large list and only ask for things you are really struggling with.*

4. *Before you go to bed, call at least six to nine Angels at your bedside and tell them to look over you and stay with you until you awake in the morning.*

They have strength and when asked to protect us they always come right away. So call on them. Some fly through the air; or swiftly glide past us. They are pure and have never lived a lifetime on earth. They have a bright, luminous light that surrounds them. They also can appear with wings, lined in different colors. There are all different levels of Angels. The Principality, being the highest Angel there is to call on when you are in desperate need. Again always feel free to call upon Angels, they will guard you.

3

YOUR NEW LIFE

I read a man who was balding. His name was Joshua, and he kept speaking negatively with me and with others about himself. When we would talk, he would constantly tell me how he would never find anyone because he was bald. I tried and tried to talk him around to saying positive things about him, but he could never allow himself to do it. He would come up with excuses and reasons why he could not do it or why it would not work for him. Well, after months of talking with him, he decided to do something about his hair loss. He went to the plastic surgeon and had a hair transplant. After spending a lot of money and going through all the pain, he still stayed negative, only now he was saying that no one would want him as soon as they found out he was a bald man so vain he had to get a hair transplant. He just could not get past this issue, and in truth, he was such a handsome man. This is a negative manifestation, but not done on purpose of course. He got his transplant but was still negative, and therefore he still had not found his kindermate. So please, speak aloud using positive words. This appears to be so easy, but this is my point. Speaking aloud, or verbal organ talk, is extremely effective and does work. You do not need any special tools.

* * * * *

Cellular Energy and Preparing Yourself

This chapter is about how manifesting works, how to clean your cellular mind memory, cellular soul memory, and how doing so will affect and improve the way you manifest positive dreams and goals.

However, each of us chooses a beginning and an ending in our contract, our learning starts in the middle. Some may think to themselves that they would like to write the middle so they do not have to go through all the rough bumps in the road on our journey. The truth is that if you wrote the middle there would be no reason to come back and be carnated over. We would all be living out our lifetime on earth perfectly. This may sound good to you and your probably asking, 'Why not Celest?' See, when we get to the otherside, remember me speaking in regards to, 'We do not feel pain, we are not jealous, we do not get sad.' Well, once we are on the otherside we do not think about the pain we experienced on earth and we want to perfect our lives. This all has to do with God, how he gives us a clean soul and a new start in life. It is up to us to prove and show the credits of our accomplishments. However, there are ways to make the middle of your contract longer and more fulfilling and positive. To be guided to the positive side and fulfill your middle of your journey.

That is the purpose of this book. In the following sections, I will tell you about mind cell memory as well as soul cell memory, and the ways to cleanse them both. Then, I will show you ways to put these same principles to work in your everyday life. Mind cell memory can affect us in so many ways. What is cellular mind memory? Mind cellular memory is when something has happened for a long enough time that it imprints itself into your mind using your mind cellular memory energy. For some of my clients this is something they have had a problem dealing with in their everyday life. Even in a positive circumstance, mind cell memories are something that occur in the present lifetime on earth. It is something that usually is of trauma or stress to our bodies and minds. For example, a woman who watches her husband get shot and killed, her mind cell memory will take in the trauma and will never forget it in this lifetime on earth. The best way to explain it is similar to a tattoo. It attaches itself on to your cells in your mind and is very hard to get rid of.

Mind Cell memory is something we deal with everyday and it is from this lifetime. Our cell memory of the mind will throw off a fear to warn or protect us. Another example: if you were to get into a car accident, it would remind you of that when you next went for a car ride. Mind cell memories will throw off a fear because it relived it in this lifetime on earth and is a way to remind you to be careful and to try to prevent this trauma from happening again.

Soul cell memory is the same thing, but it deals with past lives and the traumas of those lives. For example, I deal with this so many times as a Clairvoyant. Someone is ill and the doctor cannot diagnosis the illness. Many times it is due to a soul cell memory trauma from a past life. If someone was hung in a past life they most likely will have a fear of choking or will not let anyone touch their neck. This is a protection the cells carry from the souls energy. In the following section I will show you ways to cleanse both of these problems.

The Power of the Mind

We all know our brains are made up of living, oxygenated cells. What this means is that every complex cell within our bodies is a living breathing organism. This is a given fact, and yet too often we attach significance to the fact that the cells are sick or well. What we often fail to realize is that each cell has its own memory. This is not to say that if you get sick you should not go to a doctor. What this means is that often you can do more for whatever ails you than just going to a doctor to keep yourself healthy in mind, body and spirit.

You should think of the human body as a large city filled with many people. Now each of these people in the city has a certain job, and that job is dependent on what the city as a whole needs. It is the brain that decides what tasks need to be done.

Let me explain to you what I mean by this and how you may have already seen this in your own bodies.

I remember when I was a lot younger I had a classmate that wanted to go home early from school because she had not studied for a test that she found out was being given later in the day. She told the nurse over and over she was not feeling well, and she began faking symptoms of a cold. Not long after that, she began to actually manifest the symptoms of her imaginary cold. Therefore, she went home early that day and she ended up having a cold for the next couple of days.

There are a couple of reasons why this happened. First, her brain told her body that it had a cold so her body began to act in a way that was needed for her to defend itself against a cold. That is right; her nose began to run, and she began to run a slight temperature. The body did this because she told it to. Therefore, it gave back what she asked for.

If she verbally says aloud she is sick, again her mind cellular energies are manifesting the product...the negative product.

I am not saying all you have to do is say you are sick and you will automatically get sick. Or even that if you are already sick and you say you are healthy then you will automatically no longer be sick. However, in most of the cases I have seen over the years you will get back what you ask for.

If you strongly use verbal talk, you are feeding the mind and you will get back what you ask for. When you use negative words regarding your body, you are making it more likely that you will become sick. Let me illiterate for you what I mean with some examples from my clients.

*   *   *   *   *

I had a client named Marcy, and when she first came to me she was a diabetic. She told me that for years she had told herself that she was going to become diabetic like her father was. She told me that she said this aloud all the time to people and she had actually put herself on a diabetic diet. She told me she had done this for a few years and became diabetic shortly after. When you say something aloud and even act it out, it becomes more powerful.

*　　*　　*　　*　　*

Sometimes it will happen if you think about it often, as in the case of my client Mark.

My client, Mark, was a nurse and he worked in a hospital oncology (Cancer) department. He was very fearful that someday he would have cancer. This he attributed to the fact that he would always watch his patients die horribly and tragically from the disease and soon it began to manifest fear of it within his mind. When we talked, he told me he was even afraid to mention the word cancer and always referred to it in its clinical form. Unfortunately, before he came to me he ended up getting cancer. Before I said anything about it, he told me that he thought his own fear had manifested the cancer within him. The truth is you can manifest something just through your fear. Please remember this, even fear can manifest something.

*　　*　　*　　*　　*

If you had some simple problem like a cut finger, or a cough, you would take care of it simply by either buying cough syrup or putting a band-aid on the cut digit. At this time in our society, we have come to realize that if we let the small injuries go they can become worse. None of us wants to have a cut become infected, or a cough turn to pneumonia, so we do what we can to alleviate the problem when it is easy to do so.

When we do the little things to heal ourselves, what we are doing is nurturing the sick part of our body so that it will get better. Another way to nurture is if we have shoes that cause our feet to blister. It would only be natural not to wear those shoes anymore. All of the things I have mentioned are little things that we would do ourselves to fix the problem.

As I am doing this George wants me to tell you that these are the things we do on our own. This is not in opposition to going to a doctor or care-giver, and I always stress to my clients to seek medical advice of course. When you recognize that all these things: the finger, the cough, the blisters are all part of a living organism which needs nurturing. Well why do you not do this with your minds as well?

An example would be if you had two flower pots, and you planted a seed in both, but you only added water to one of them. While the other, you nurtured with sun and water. Which plant would thrive the most? Of course the one with the sun and water. My point is your mind also needs the full degree of nurturing in order to give you back everything you need. Why feed the mind only half of what it is suppose to get? It is just like only giving the seed water and no sun. So many of us fail to see this. We seem to think we need some magic pill when it all is so simple to get back what you ask for in this journey.

There are many times when there is a small problem with our minds that we can fix ourselves. Unfortunately, people tend to neglect the mind, and most of the time they do not even realize it. We do this at least twenty to thirty times a day or more. Nurturing your mind is the main key to getting what you want from life.

I am going to talk to you about cellular energy as opposed to chemical energy. Cellular energy is something you give to your mind that would seed positive energy to your brain cells. The difference is that chemical is an illness. When that happens, it would require the seeking of a doctor to correct the chemical imbalance. This would be for those that are bi-polar or schizophrenic and so on. With cellular energy of the mind, we would speak out verbally to it so as to nurture it and improve it.

With chemical problems, you would see a doctor and he would prescribe the necessary medicine to fix it. Even then you can also incorporate the positive cellular energy through positive manifestation techniques later described in the health section of this book. I am trying to teach you how to manifest positive energy. If you follow the steps I will show you, then you will be ready to cleanse your soul cell memory, mind cell memory and to positively manifest your dreams and goals into reality.

4

CLEANSING YOUR HOME AND BODY

Ouija Boards

[Note: By no means is the author or publisher claiming the creators, producers, manufactures or consumers who own Ouija Boards to be evil spirits or dark entities. For the purpose of this book, Ouija Boards are likened to that of antiques in the fact they can attract certain spirits, and is not a reflection of the board itself. In addition, the name Ouija Boards is a generalization, and not a comment of a specific product, trademark, or copyright.]

There are two things you need to take care of prior to performing any manifestation, as well as to help you with your own personal cleansing.

The first is to get rid of any Ouija boards that you may have in your house or apartment. A good spirit never uses a board; evil spirits always run them. It may seem to be an innocent game, but in truth, it is not. I have seen Ouija boards sold in toy stores, and bought by parents for their children, without a single thought as to who or what is running these boards.

When the board is first used, it sends out a call to whatever nearest evil entity is willing to answer. It is not an Angel, Spirit Guide, or even a crossed-over loved one that answers the call of the board, it is always an evil spirit.

Once that evil spirit knows that there is someone willing to listen to them then they will hang around that person's life until they are used over and over again. The evil entity could be a soul that has refused to crossover due to its fear of repercussions on the otherside or it could be a demonic spirit that has forsaken the light. Either way, I have never seen or even heard of a person having a good life with a Ouija board in their house.

A Ouija board in and of itself is not made up of evil material, but once completed the board has a natural inclination towards evil and it will actively attempt to find an evil entity. This entity may give the user good advice simply to entice them to further use. Then it will begin to twist the user to its own ends, which is never good. It would do this so it could cause them greater harm later on when they come to rely on it. However, there is also a chance that when the user asks it for something the dark entity will tell them an answer for no other reason but to harm or trick you.

Before you do anything with manifesting, it is imperative that you destroy the board so no one else can use it. Even if you have a board that you have never used before, or have not used in a long time, then you still need to get rid of it. The reason for that is that every dark entity wants desperately for you to go back to the board to use it again to try to solve your problems. In addition, dark entities are desperate to get attention from those that have let them into their lives. A dark entity will do anything to get someone to pay attention to them. Unlike entities of the light, dark entities do not care about you or your loved ones. They have no desire to see your soul ascending forward; all they care about are themselves. They are plainly negative and evil. They are tricksters and take their only joy in tormenting others.

I had a client that was always coming to me with problems and every time one would get fixed another would take its place right after. During a reading, I read that he had a Ouija board. He told me that the board told him that some of his friends as well as himself would be passing over soon.

Please note that no spirit guide or angel will tell you that you are going to die. They never use the word die. They may tell you that you need to see a doctor immediately during a reading or tell the psychic the client will pass away without immediate medical attention. I always confront a client or their loved ones during a reading if my spirit guide George feels they are ill, but they cannot circumvent free will.

The following are the steps you need to follow to get rid of a Ouija board, and rid the evil entity. Please remember to do it exactly this way.

1) Say, "God please protect me with your white light from the Holy Spirit."

2) Go outside with the Ouija board and place the board in a metal garbage can or something metal that is non-flammable. Please be careful you do not burn yourself.

3) Burn the board completely to ashes.

4) As the board is burning, dig a hole at least 1 foot down and 1 foot across.

5) Place the ashes in the hole.

6) After placing the ashes in the hole, place the pendulum in the hole with it. Do not forget to bury the pendulum; it was a focus point for the evil entity.

Do not bury these things on your property. You should go to a natural site like an open field or something like it. I had a client once put the ashes in a flowerpot because it was too difficult to dig during the wintertime. This does not work.

Cleansing You Home

The second thing for you to do is to cleanse you house or apartment. Cleansing your house is important because until you do, the negative energy that may have been there will block any attempts by you to bring in good energy. Many people that have a new house call upon me when they are troubled by doors slamming, or beds shaking. I do not make a habit of exorcising entities from homes. It requires a lot of energy from me and if I become too tired, the ghost in the home may actually follow me home. They would rather stay where they are at because it is a comfort zone. There are many reasons for this. One is, before they died they may of murdered their spouse or what have you and they are still angry, stuck, stubborn, did not want to leave or didn't think they were dead or still may not think they are dead.

When I perform this task, I will make sure I am well rested as I do in my readings before I talk to the entity and ask them to leave the premises and go to be with God. Nine times out of ten, the ghost simply refuses to accept that they are dead. When that is the case, I simply have to convince them that it is their time to move on; and accept the fact that their life here is over and they need to go to the otherside. I always call upon the white light from the Holy Spirit before, during, and after. Many houses I have done are those that have had trouble selling and there is often a "For Sale" sign up in the front yard. After I talk with the ghost, it will not be long before the sign is taken down and the property is attractive to others again.

A house can be haunted or troubled even if it is new; because of something you bring home, like from a garage sale or antique sale. Even old wood that is being used to rebuild a new deck will carry the spirit with it to the new destination.

Everything carries energy from those around it, or events around it. If you bring something used into your house or apartment, it is highly possible you are bringing home something that absorbed a ghost or entity filled with negative energy, just like a sponge. Only when we pick up those things that have negative energy do we really need to concern ourselves with. Therefore, feel the energy and try to tune in to see if it does not feel good. For instance, someone who unpacked oranges in the grocery store may have been a very negative person and you will bring the orange home which absorbed the negative energy from that individual.

If you move into a place that is not good, you will feel

tired and restless for the whole time you are there. Understand that these feelings always occur at some time in life but it will be persistent if you do not cleanse your apartment or house. In addition, you will find yourself having more troubles than before when you make big changes in your life. By troubles I mean, if you lose your job or someone dies, or something like that. Here are a few items you will need to properly cleanse your living area:

- · Buy some sea salt. This can be purchased at any health food store. The price is fairly minimal.
- · A spray bottle. Any dollar store or department store will carry these.
- · Sagestick or smudgestick. You can get this at a metaphysical store or online. I prefer white sage, as it is what I use to cleanse my house.

Once you have these items you are ready to cleanse your place. Everything in your house has energy, even the dust. When cleaning your house, make sure you always clean from bottom to top. In addition, it would be advantageous if you were to move all furniture slightly away from the walls in your home. It does not have to be to far away, just enough that you can get the spray bottle behind it.

Then take your spray bottle and fill it with clean water, tap water is acceptable. After the bottle is full, place within the water a teaspoon of the sea salt. Now shake the contents thoroughly.

Then, around your house or apartment spray a fine mist at all four corners of the walls in every room. If you live in a house, you must always start outside first, and then go inside. If it is cold bundle up. Be sure, once you start you do not stop until it has been done. If you do, there is a chance that you will break up the protection and allow negativity to come back in.

Next, do the same thing with the doors. You want to go through each room and spray from the bottom to the top. Remember if you have multiple levels you start in the basement and work your way through to the attic.

After that is complete, you want to open each window in your house/apartment at least two inches. This will allow negative energy to leave.

Light your sagestick; make sure it is well lit, so the top is always smoking. It is best to always carry a lighter just in case the smoldering goes out. That would break the cleansing process.

Take your sage stick and move in each room, blowing the smoke lightly to every corner of the walls just like you did with the salt water mixture. Remember to do this in each room and at every door and window.

Do the same thing with every corner of the house if you have an attached garage then you will want to do that as well. For safety's sake, remember do not blow on the embers. You only want to blow on the smoke itself. If for some reason you are unable to keep the stick going constantly, make sure to keep a lighter handy. If the smoke stops, it is important to for you to also stop where it happened and relight the stick at the point of stoppage. After the first half hour, you may close the windows. This will give the negative energy time to leave your dwelling.

After that is done, you are ready to cleanse yourself. To do this you are going to need to remove all your clothes and run a bath for yourself.

As the tub is filling, place at least ½ cup of sea salt/ocean salt in the water.

After you have filled the tub so it will not overflow when you get in, you will stand on a sure surface and relight the sage stick.

Making sure to keep the stick away from your body, you will first move it toward your forehead, also think of this as your third eye. If the smoke begins to get into your eyes close them and move the stick further away from your body.

You will then move the stick over to your right ear, and

then your left.

Re-center the stick and slowly bring it down your body allowing the smoke to envelope you. Being very careful not to touch yourself with the stick, you will want to spread your legs and carefully wave the stick under your groin area.

Bring the stick as far as you can down the rest of your body. Trying to make sure you get down to the soles of your feet.

Then soak in the tub for half an hour. This cleanses and detoxifies you from negative energy.

When you are done get out of the tub and stand up and watch the water go down the drain. As it does say aloud, "I am now flushing down negative energy." As the water goes down the drain, imagine just that.

You should do this bathing and personal sage at least once every 2 months. You do not have to do the house cleaning except for once every other season. On the other hand, if you are a psychic or medium, or even if you are trying to bring out whatever psychic abilities you may have, then you need to do this every week. You should do the house cleansing every other month.

The sixth chakra is referred to as the Third Eye. It is located above the physical eyes on the center of the forehead. This is the center for psychic ability, higher intuition, the energies of spirit and light. It also assists in the purification of negative tendencies and in the elimination of selfish attitudes. Through the power of the sixth chakra, you can receive guidance, channel, and tune into your Higher Self.

When this chakra is not balanced, you may feel non-assertive, afraid of success, or go the opposite way and be egotistical. Physical symptoms may include headaches, blurred vision, blindness, and eyestrain.

Reiki

Another way to help cleanse the imprint of negativity that has been placed on your soul, from negative talk or being around negative energies is Reiki. Reiki will cleanse your body and organs. It will also keep them balanced and cleansed with positive energy.

Reiki (pronounced Ray-Key) is a method of natural healing based on the application of Universal Life Force Energy. Reiki literally means Universal Life Force Energy. Reiki is one of the more widely known forms of energy healing. Energy Healing involves direct application of Chi for the purpose of strengthening the client's energy system. Chi is a term for the underlying force the universe is made of. All cultures have talked about the physical universe being made of an underlying form of something. Modern physics research is now coming to understand the universe is made of energy, which is subject to, or affected by, thought.

Imagine the implications of the universe around us made from energy, which can be shaped and manipulated by thoughts. Both Quantum Physics and ancient Metaphysics have come to this same conclusion. This makes some things easy to understand, such as miraculous cures, or exotic diseases that have no apparent physical cause.

The way we acquire deviations from our ideal form is to accept limitations into our life. Most of this comes from early childhood because that is the phase of life where we are the most open and inquisitive about life. A limitation may be a parent yelling, *"BE QUIET!"* enough times that the child learns to not speak. Another limitation may be a limp that continues longer after the physical injury has healed, maybe with phantom pains. These limitations are behavior patterns, eating patterns, physical limitations, imagined physical limitations, psychological, mental, or emotional ways of being, living, expressing or loving that is not in alignment with our personal highest expression.

In any healing the goal is to find the limitation, recognize the pattern, recognize where it came from, and let it go. Reiki accomplishes this by providing the recipient enough energy to step above (metaphorically) to see all that and have the courage to let go. This usually does not happen consciously as a result of Reiki, but sometimes it does happen that Reiki gives the recipient the conscious awareness of the pattern and recognizing where it came from.

Our lives are a constant flow of patterns of activity, such as the pattern used to accomplish eating breakfast, and it is our choice to have these patterns remain stuck in limited expression, or to release the old patterns and try on new and shinier ones. Reiki stimulates our cells and organs and keeps its blocks from forming meaning. Our bodies will be recharged and able to function more properly from stress. If you have a water hose and you put a kink in it you will not get a water flow when you turn the water on. Reiki acts in a similar way. It takes the blocks out of our energy flow so our body can operate properly. I happen to do my Reiki different with every individual person. It all depends on what may be making them ill. I use a different technique of healing for each client. My Spirit Guide George tells me what technique to use on every client.

My cat Trexie has had terrible problems with her bowels. She is unable to move them. Medications were not working so I performed Reiki on her. She is not having any problems at all currently. Animals have a soul and benefit from Reiki also. Another example is recently I had very low Blood Pressure, in fact extremely low. The moment I preformed Reiki on myself, I elevated my Blood Pressure and it is now staying at a normal range. By all means this is not to be used in the place of a doctor, however it is very effective and many doctors I work with are sending there patients to a Reiki master.

Reiki is also a gateway, shining pure love into the universe. It is this love that allows us to transcend our wounds and help us remember our true nature.

Reiki has a unique history. The many books on Reiki give similar histories of, and these are summarized below. I do not pretend to be an authority on the History of Reiki. Instead of spending much effort debating the past and the exact path by which Reiki came to us, I find it more fruitful to use the energy and experience the truth of the larger reality of all that is. This is not to say that the history is unimportant. As human beings, we tend to react based on the past so it is natural to want to know where things come from.

With roots in Japan prior to World War II, it is not surprising that some documentation was lost. Apparently, the survivors of Dr. Hayashi lost to the war the resources allowing them to continue the clinic he founded and perhaps stopped practicing Reiki. If it were not for Mrs. Takata, learning Reiki before the war and bringing it to America, this healing technique could well have been lost to the world. It is almost a miracle in itself how close we came to losing Reiki. Of course, we perhaps lost some valuable memories, knowledge and continuity had the lineage not been squeezed through one person. We can only hope that practice, study and intuition will bring back any lost knowledge and practices.

Lost knowledge, particularly the evidence to support the following history, does give rise to possible skepticism. Still, Reiki speaks for itself on every use. The energy is real and easily experienced. Once one has experienced the energy, particularly if one is an attuned Reiki practitioner, it is always there and easily demonstrates its truth. Whatever the truth and reality of the claims in the history given below, the ability to perform Reiki so easily came from somewhere and is, for me, the ultimate proof that this path of development is wise.

It was discovered by Dr. Usui in the late 1800's, a teacher or perhaps dean of a Christian school in Japan.

During these travels, he met Dr. Chujiro Hayashi, a Naval Commander in the Naval Reserve. He came from a well educated and well to-do family. He met Dr. Usui in the marketplace holding a lit torch announcing his lecture at a nearby temple.

Dr. Hayashi was very impressed with the sincerity and conviction of Dr. Usui. When asked by Usui to accompany him in his travels, Dr. Hayashi agreed. Moreover, they traveled around teaching and healing. After Dr. Usui passed on, Dr. Hayashi became the leader of Reiki.

Dr. Hayashi opened a clinic in Tokyo near the Imperial Palace. It consisted of eight beds in a large room, two practitioners per patient. One would treat the head and the other would be on the right treating the stomach area, then both would treat the patients back. The practitioners all worked here doing healings. They would also go to the homes of sick people for house calls.

To become a Reiki Practitioner in that time, one had to be accepted by the masters in the Reiki organization, and second had to promise to use Reiki daily and volunteer some hours to practice Reiki regularly in the clinic.

Dr. Hayashi passed on Tuesday, May 10, 1940. This was just prior to World War II and it was clear that Japan would enter the war. Being a Reserve Officer, Dr. Hayashi knew he would be recalled to duty and therefore become responsible for killing many people. This he did not want to do, and so determined to end his life. In addition he wished to, and did, pass leadership over to Reiki to Mrs. Takata, perhaps because she would not be in Japan and therefore relatively safe and able to continue the practice.

Mrs. Hawayo Takata was born in Hawaii, on Kauai, on Christmas Eve 1900 of Japanese descent. In the 1930's, she went to Japan to visit her family there, and inform them of the death of her sister. While there, she became very sick and was in the hospital. The doctors were going to operate, and as she was being prepared, she kept hearing a voice saying "Operation not necessary." Eventually she jumped off the table asking, "Is there another way?" The doctor had a sister who had been cured of dysentery at Dr. Hayashi's clinic and suggested to Mrs. Takata she talk with his sister. The sister brought Mrs. Takata to the clinic and her treatments there began.

After Mrs. Takata became well she wanted to learn this for herself. However, Dr. Hayashi was not willing to teach her because she was a foreigner. Through the good graces of her doctor, Mrs. Takata was able to persuade Dr. Hayashi to train her in Reiki. This training took a year and brought her to what we would now call Reiki Level II. She could do everything but train other practitioners.

After this year, she returned to Hawaii. In Hawaii, she also learned the lesson of having the recipient perceive value in receiving treatments. She treated a neighbor but did not charge, this neighbor did not value the treatments and did not become well. She treated another relative and this time charged, and this relative did stay well. Thus, the tradition of charging for Reiki treatment was reinforced.

In November 1936, Dr. Hayashi came to Hawaii for a speaking tour to promote Reiki. During this time, he trained Mrs. Takata to teach Reiki, thus making her what we now would call a Reiki Master. As he left Hawaii, he asked her to come to see him when he summoned her.

After some more time, it was nearing when World War II would start, the part in Europe already having begun. Dr. Hayashi appeared to Mrs. Takata in a dream asking her to come to Japan. She did this and found Dr. Hayashi having his Naval Uniform out of storage and fretful. With the coming war, he knew it was a matter of time before the Navy would call him out of retirement and he would be asked to perform actions he was not capable of doing due to his spiritual development. At this time, he passed to Mrs. Takata the leadership of Reiki. He gathered all the Reiki Masters to a gathering, announced Mrs. Takata to be the leader of Reiki, and then announced he would kill his physical body through bursting three blood vessels. In addition, as he continued speaking and lecturing those blood vessels burst and he died.

Mrs. Takata returned to Hawaii and continued using and teaching Reiki. Eventually she moved to California, using and teaching Reiki there as well. She did not teach other masters until 1975, and before her own death in 1980, she trained 22 Reiki Masters.

Reiki is easily learned, simple to use, and beneficial for all. It is one of many forms of healing through the use of the natural forces. A Reiki healing is very simply performed. The practitioner places his or her hand upon the person to be healed with the intent for healing to occur, and then the energy begins flowing. The Reiki energy is smart since the Universe is a very smart place indeed. The energy knows where to go, and what to do once it gets there, or else is being directed by a higher intelligence. The energy manages its own flow to and within the recipient. It draws through the healer exactly that amount of energy that the recipient needs. All this happens without direct conscious intervention by the healer. The healer's job is to get out of the way, to keep the healing space open, and to watch and listen for signs of what to do next.

You relax, fully clothed, on a couch or seated while the healer holds his hands on or above you. A treatment can last an hour or longer depending on the treatment required. In the western world, many practitioners use the standard hand positions and commonly a full treatment is given covering all the important organs of the body.

No pressure is placed on the body, making it ideal for treating all ages and conditions. Sometimes hands are even held away from the body. The energy flows wherever it is required (spiritually guided) and can normally be felt as a warm sensation or tingling in the body. Receiving Reiki is a very relaxing and soothing experience.

Reiki is a powerful and gentle healing technique that:

- Strengthens the immune system
- Adjusts to the natural needs of the receiver
- Heals holistically
- Clears toxins
- Promotes creativity
- Relieves pain
- Relaxes and reduces stress
- Treats warning signs and causes of illness
- Enhances personal awareness
- Balances the energies in the body
- Aids meditation and positive thinking
- Releases blocked and suppressed feelings
- Balances the organs and glands
- Encourages natural self-healing

Reiki is capable of healing almost anything because it works at the very fundamental levels of reality. Even though the capability is there, this is not what always happens. The limits to Reiki seem to be in the recipient's willingness to cast off old habits and patterns, to accept change and to accept healing. The level of reality where Reiki operates is the underlying energy structure of matter, as the physical matter we see around us is a solidified form of energy. Emotional difficulties are just as healable as physical ones since emotional issues are even more directly present in the energy structures.

In this context, the word Healing has a somewhat different meaning from the widely accepted meaning. The widely accepted meaning for healing seems to be curing of symptoms, for that seems to be what medical doctors and the like look to do in their practice. The other meaning for healing, used in the practice of Reiki as well as other related areas, is the return to greater wholeness. There is an ideal form each of us has, this ideal form being the highest and clearest expression of who we are. Pain or disease comes from any deviation between the person's current form in the 3D physical world and this ideal form. Healing then, is to bring this physical form into closer alignment with the ideal form.

Crystals

The reason for using crystals is to arrange the energy within your body. Crystals allow the bad energy to be taken out of your body and then place positive energy in it. It is best to use a clear quartz crystal when first starting. As you become more proficient with the use of crystals, you can experiment with all the other myriad colors and types. You can purchase crystals on line or at any metaphysical store.

Many users of crystals carry them around with them

throughout the day. It is important to know that if you choose to wear a crystal around your neck on a chain of some type that you not put a hole through the crystal. You need to place the crystal in a pouch or tie around it or hold it in the palm of your hands. When you feel negative, or are around someone negative, place a clear quartz in the palm of your hand. It absorbs negative energy from you, which you are getting from others around you. I always advise others to hold the clear quartz in the palm of their hand when they are working in large crowds. Such as seminars, while they are conducting for instance. It is important to have the stones next to your body or to your skin, rather than in your pocket. Some people will simply carry it around them in their jeans pocket or in the breast pocket of their shirts.

Sometimes a stone or crystal you are strongly drawn to does not feel good, or a stone that felt good previously does not feel good now. The stone or crystal may need to be cleansed. Clearing is important before using any stone for healing. The clearer the energy of a healing stone, the more powerful it is. Crystals need to be cleansed as soon as they are purchased as well as clearing after every healing. A cleansed ready crystal feels positive and bright, tingly and cold to the touch. A crystal that needs clearing may feel hot, heavy or drained.

Remember they absorb our negative energies, which can make us sick, emotionally or physically. There are a number of ways to effectively clear crystals and gemstones.

Smudging

A fast and easy way to cleanse your crystals is to smudge them with burning sage. Smudging is an excellent way to make sure your stones are purified. Simply hold the burning sage stick while passing your stone through the smoke. Again, I prefer white sage, not cedar. You can use the same sage you used for cleansing your house earlier. It is sometimes best to do this a couple of times just to make sure of a good cleansing.

Another method of cleansing your crystals or quartz is to fill a cup of sea salt and water and let the crystals soak in the mixture for a few hours. If you are in a hurry, you can take them out as soon as one hour. I do recommend letting them soak all night while you are sleeping. I recommend you doing this sea soak at least once a week or as often as you wish. If you are using the crystals just for yourself 1-2 times a week is fine to do cleansings, however if you are using the crystals for Reiki, always cleanse them after each person you use them on immediately.

Another way to cleanse your crystals is to do a holy water soak. This is the same method as the sea salt. Except that you are using Holy water. By the way, I always recommend having holy water in your house or apartment. Keep it in a spray bottle and mist yourself and your house or apartment when you feel negative or just sluggish.

Never use warm or hot water when doing a physical cleaning of your crystal. Whenever you are holding your crystal or inspecting it for whatever reason be sure to see the crystal as tingly, gleaming, fresh and connected to you.

After you have chosen and cleared your crystal, it is a good idea to dedicate it or program it. The purpose of programming a crystal is to focus its abilities on something you specifically need, thereby magnifying the stone's intent through your own. A crystal or stone that is planned and committed in these ways becomes more powerful and useful as a tool. It is always best to use a professional when it comes to dealing with the internal energies that are within your body.

The method of using crystals on the receiver's body for healing is called laying on of stones. It is a powerful method of cleansing negative energy, clearing and harmonizing the Chakras, effecting emotional release, and bringing light and healing into body. Cleared, programmed, and dedicated stones move the receiver's vibration into alignment with the planet and the universal web. This results in a freeing of life force energy in the Chakras and aura, a healing of the Body of Light, and a transformation of negative or disease into health.

A laying on of stones healing can be quite intense. There is frequently a key energy swing during this style of healing. Recurrent emotional discharges, past life and this life trauma breaks may occur whenever this is attempted successfully. The healer's function in this is to pause for the discharge to end and to be completely tolerant. When the session is over, there may also be a physical detoxification progression that can continue for up to a week. Be aware of what is happening, and allow it. The changes are always positive and are usually gentle. I also have seen my clients become a little fidgety but this will not last long, a few hours only. This can occur when your body really needed to be cleansed and is in sort of a shock until it adjusts from getting rid of all the heavy negative energies it was holding. Always remember to drink plenty of water after you have a Reiki treatment, so you flush out the impurities that Reiki released.

Meditation and Cellular Mind Memory

The biggest problem you may face in overcoming your negative mind cellular energy is fear; fear of failure, fear of success, fear of unworthiness. In truth, it is these internal fears that may keep you from maintaining your positive energy. Through the means of meditation, you can train your mind to set aside your fears and concerns. Meditation enables you to strengthen your mind to overcome your fears so that they do not hamper you.

Meditation is just one aspect you can use to help facilitate your manifesting positive energy. For some people, learning to focus the mind and relax the body helps them to find that the things they want to manifest will come to fruition easier and with better clarity than without.

Meditation helps to cleanse the mind. In the last sections, I showed you ways to cleanse your body and soul. This section is about the why and how to cleanse your mind. I will start with the internal workings of the mind and then move towards the biological.

There are techniques in meditation where you are instructed to concentrate on the tip of your nose, on your breathing, on your movements, to think of something, repeat a mantra or repeat some affirmations. In all of these methods, you are actually teaching the mind to stick to one object, action or thought. You are training it to become focused on one thing.

You can sit by the sea and watch the waves, follow a cloud in the sky, concentrate on a subject and try to understand it. You can repeat a prayer or think about God. These too are all various methods of meditation. The main theme of them all is focusing the mind on one subject, in other words, concentration. Do not make it something difficult to do. Do any form you feel comfortable with, however, I prefer just sitting and not thinking. This will clear your mind and is very simple to do. It will recharge your mind, and the cells in your brain. You don't need any fancy equipment like mats or shoes or special clothing, just be comfortable.

The mind is usually restless. By disciplining its waves, it becomes quiet. When the mind is quiet, the body is quiet too. Meditation is not different from any other method of training. To succeed, you need perseverance, inner strength, ambition and faith. To gain results, you need to devote, time, energy and love. We all need to clear our minds, which will in-turn nurture our minds and that is a big step in preparing for positive manifestation.

Meditation helps to develop physical and mental calmness, concentration, memory, insight, internal strength and peace of mind. It may also lead to spiritual enlightenment. It depends on how enthusiastic you are, and how much energy and time you devote to it.

If you persevere and practice with sincerity and deliberation, you become able to silence your fears. When the mind becomes naturally quiet, you find out who you really are, and what it is you truly want. When you have been able to set aside your fears it becomes so much easier to manifest what you truly want, because you know what it is you do want.

The first thing you always want to do no matter what exercise you are attempting, be it meditation or Reiki or crystals, is to surround yourself with the white light. When in doubt always, surround yourself in white light from the Holy Spirit.

First, envision that you have a bright white light in the center of your being. This white light is something that should feel warm and comforting to you. The light itself should be almost a blindingly white, almost like the sun on a very clear summer day at noon. I like to place the light where my heart is. From there, imagine the light expanding and infusing to each part of your body. Starting from the center of your chest between your breasts, imagine the light going from mid-chest, up toward your head and at the same time down your legs, then from your chest at the same time out to each arm. Like the shape of a cross. Then, imagine from the top of your head to the bottom of your feet, you are closing yourself into this white light, sealing it around you. Be sure to seal it at the top of your head and your feet almost like when someone is blowing glass. They start at one point and seal it off completely. Eventually, the light has encircled your whole body. After you are done, within your minds eye, you will see a perfectly sealed oblong ball of white light surrounding you from all angles. It should be radiating outwards a few feet.

The root chakra is located at the base of the spine at the tailbone in back, and the pubic bone in front. This center holds the basic needs for survival, security and safety. The root chakra is powerfully related to our contact with the Earth; providing us with the ability to be grounded to the earth. This is also the center of manifestation.

When you are trying to make things happen in the material world, business or material possessions, the energy to succeed will come from the first chakra.

If this chakra is blocked an individual may feel fearful, anxious, insecure and frustrated. Problems like obesity, anorexia nervosa, and knee troubles can occur. Root body parts include the hips, legs, lower back and sexual organs.

NOTE: A man's sexual organs are located primarily in his first chakra, so male sexual energy is usually experienced primarily as physical. A woman's sexual organs are located primarily in her second chakra, so female sexual energy is usually experienced primarily as emotional. Both chakras are associated with sexual energy.

What you want to do is when you wake and you have done your morning ritual of brushing your teeth, showering, shaving, bathroom duties etc, place the white light around you then. After that, it is important to say the following out-loud, "God protect me with the white light from the Holy Spirit. Keep me from receiving and giving negativity." I have found this works best if said three times in a row. Then, also use the method I mentioned with you extending white light from your chest to your head and feet then from chest to both arms in the shape of a cross. All this is done at the same time, and then seal yourself from head to toe in a bright light dome.

If you do not do this in the morning, then as you go through the day, you run the risk of having a negative person affect you that day. When you do this, it almost creates a protective aura around your body. To let you know, an aura surrounds someone anywhere from four inches to couple of feet out. It always varies how much someone's aura comes out from their body. This is important to know because even if you say to yourself, 'I am not going to let their negativity affect me.' The truth is, their aura can still be close enough to you to attach itself to your aura and negatively affect it. By doing so, that would defeat the purpose of following the procedures I have given you.

Positive Cellular Talk

Positive cellular talk is what you will use to help manifest the positive aspects of your life. It is also a key to cleansing you of negative energy.

Every night, you should take just a minute of your time to do the following exercise. When you lay your head on your pillow before sleep, say out load, "God please erase my negative cell memory," in regards to whatever is bothering you. You will not get it out of your memory completely, but it will eventually get better. If you are having a problem with a phobia, then you will need to do this every night prior to going to sleep. It may only take a couple of nights but I have seen this type of cleansing take weeks. Remember it does not rid you completely of the problem. If for some reason you cannot do this in bed before sleep, then another way is to sit in a quiet darkened area.

The following sections contain the crucial points to making sure that your positive cellular talk works throughout your lifetime. It is important for you to implement the following steps into your everyday life.

Get the Proper Sleep

You have to realize that when you talk aloud you first give it to your mind. For positive manifestation, you need to nurture the mind so that it can accept the positive verbal talk. If you speak aloud, you are giving it to the mind. Although, if your mind is not filled properly with oxygenated cells, then the mind will have problems accepting what you are trying to manifest. So, prior to starting your manifestation, make sure you have had the proper amount of sleep you need. Proper sleep is an important tool in many ways. However, for positive manifesting it is a crucial aspect. If your mind has not recharged properly through sleep, then it will not be able to manifest properly. Every person has their own personal amount of sleep that they require. In addition, this number actually changes with age. I have known many people that have needed as few as four hours of sleep and some as much as ten. If you attempt to use positive cellular talk or even manifesting without accepting this first rule, then I would give you a slim chance of actually succeeding.

Stay Away From Negative Energy

This comes from other people as well as the things around you. Remember the white light that you placed around you in the earlier chapter? The fact is, everyone and everything has something like that around him or her all the time. When you place that white light around you, it is as if you have changed your aura for one that is pure and upbeat, you have strengthened it. As the day progresses, your light begins to counteract with everything that is around you. You will find that as you interact with more people that are close to your white light, the longer you will be able to maintain the light you have placed around you. The light is sealed around your body and keeps negative energy from entering, almost as if you were in a bubble, protected. The light will shoot out a few feet and even though others can walk close to you, their negative energy cannot penetrate you. White light is very powerful.

I think the best analogy I can give you would be this: If you put half a dozen buckets of water filled to the top in the back of a truck. Then you drive down a very bumpy, windy road. By the end of the trip, the buckets would have splashed over into each of the other buckets. That is the same way with life. No matter how you start your day, by the end of it everything and everyone that you have come in contact with you has splashed their light into yours. That being the case, if you find yourself in a situation where you are at lunch and the person you are eating with talks constantly about how terrible their health is you are being negatively effected by their own negative cellular talk. Even though you are not saying these things yourself it still affects you, because you are hearing it. When you hear things like this type of negative energy you process it in your mind. Their negative energy is coming onto you. This happens especially if your mind is not focused and it has not been properly cleansed and recharged.

Do Not Let Others Guide You Negatively

This is a crucial one. Of all the relationships you enter into, this is the one that you need to be the most careful of. My spirit guide has told me this is the most crucial one. I have done many readings for people and this is the most common problem clients have. It usually is a spouse, teacher, parent, or child that is doing this and usually they do not do this with malice or intent. When someone tells you that you are no good at something or you will not succeed at something, this can affect your cellular energy strongly. If for one reason or another you find that you cannot simply tell them to stop or walk away from them, I want you to excuse yourself from them and go to the bathroom or someplace where you are alone and close your eyes and re-envision the white light around you, and say, "I am rejecting all negative energy that comes to me." Repeat this a couple of times. If you know that you will be having negative energy coming to you at a meeting or lunch then it will be a good idea to do this just prior to the meeting.

It is important to understand the difference between constructive criticism and negative criticism. If someone is trying to teach you a better way of doing what you are doing, it is a good idea to listen. If what they say makes sense then incorporate that into your routine.

Do Not Talk Negatively About Yourself

This is fairly self-explanatory. Basically what this means is do not put yourself down. Do not:

- Claim that you are going to get sick, before you do get sick.
- Say you cannot do something that you can do.
- Call yourself derogatory names, such as stupid, idiot, unlucky, etc.
- If you are unsure whether you can complete a task, do not say you will fail.

If you say something negative then right away, say, " Cancel." You must say it aloud. If you do not, then here is what can happen. You have said this negative thing and it becomes a small imprint in your memory, and the longer you take to cancel, the more cells pick the negative up. When you say it right away, it cleanses the immediate cells affected and because it has not had time to truly ingrain into the cell, it is almost like it never happened.

As an example of this, consider the following. Think of your cell as a tree and when you say negative things, it is like a parasite that becomes attached to the tree. When you say cancel right away, the parasite has not gotten the chance to infect the tree. It will scar the surface a little, but as long as you do not inject more parasites in it, then it will be fine.

On the other hand, if you wait around to say it, then you have given the parasite the time it needs to take the opportunity to get under the skin or bark of the tree. Then even though you have said cancel, later it may kill the parasite but the damage has been partly done and it has slowly begun to create a disease within the tree. Every time that diseased cell comes in contact with a healthy cell, it rubs the disease off onto it.

This is important to know for when you cleanse yourself in the morning, and also for the few times a year when you do a complete cleansing. Each cell thinks, feels, and breathes. When we connect with our soul cell memory, we are connecting to all of our past lives and mind cell memory of our present lives. We can tap into the causes for our pain and our feelings. I have had many clients over the years that have had nothing medically wrong with them and yet they will be in pain. Another thing that is medically proven is that when we are in pain our blood pressure rises. These are the things that lead me to believe that illnesses are not just medically driven and there is something within them, which is driven internally in their cell memory.

Our soul has been reincarnated over many times and with each time there has been many problems we have encountered; relationships, health, money, fears, or trauma. With in our cells these things still exist and we can tap into that cell memory. You have to understand, the variables of problems are almost infinite. Everything we have done that affected our past lives. For example, maybe someone was homeless in a past life. Then they get carnated over and they may become very paranoid about their money…afraid to go without. In turn they may become a workaholic because their soul cell memory is still living it. The soul has a memory. Please note, that the soul memory is different than the brain or mind cell memory. The soul that wrote the contract is saying to the mind, "Let's make a move on this. We are behind on the contract." So the soul that wrote the contract is leaving it up to us; our minds and body, to manifest what the soul wrote in the contract. The amount of variables is infinite and by cleansing and getting in touch with those soul cell memories, we can see possible ways of fixing our current problems. Always try to cure everything that is troubling you in this lifetime on Earth so that you do not take it with you. If not, then the next lifetime you will have this soul cell memory problem because you did not fix it in the last lifetime.

Some people have had a limb amputated and even years later can feel as if at times the limb is still attached. This can occur in the present lifetime and your last lifetime. If it occurs in the present lifetime you will feel you still have a limb, but if it was a past life, a soul cell memory, you may worry you could lose your limb and not know why you have this fear. In this lifetime the mind cell memory is still there. Doctors call this a phantom memory. Our mind cell memory never forgets. This includes our past lives. Our souls know everything about our past lives; how we lived and how we died. It is not like our minds that remember only one life and even then only in a selective and sketchy way. When we are born, our souls implant onto our cells some of the problems or even good things from our past life. This is why some people fear something for no apparent reason, or it can also explain déjà vu, as well as some other things. A young woman has a fear of a certain park, it may be that in a past life she was raped and killed in the park. If someone goes to a doctor when they are forty and they complain of a throat problem, sometimes the doctor may find nothing wrong with them. Well the problem may be caused by a past life. It is understandable, especially if in a past life at the same age they had contracted throat cancer.

This is not a knock against the medical profession. It is simply that they are not trained to deal with past life problems. However, I found more and more the medical profession is understanding it and open to it, which makes me very happy. In fact, the person with the sore throat could have negatively manifested the same problem from a past life and actually still end up with an actual throat problem now. Even to the point to where they still need a doctor's assistance. The problems with that are twofold; first, when you say it or feel it you are sending out to the universal energy. Second, you create a complex cell memory; one that was implanted from your soul and then reinforced from you with negative soul cell energy. Usually this comes from the nearest past life. Unless, the former life before it was so traumatic it can actually leap over the lives before it and even affect multiple lives until you cure it. If you feel you have been in a place before then you probably have. In the other lives you had been there before.

My Spirit Guide tells me that animals do not reincarnate they are pure souls and have no need to come back over. When they cross over they are looked after by spirit guides.

If you need to go see a psychic, then check around first. Get positive feedback from friends or family. Find out what they say is happening; do not be afraid to ask questions about their methods and beliefs. There are a good number of fake psychic's out there that just want to take your money. A true psychic is what she is and to be anything else is a waste. If you have any pets keep them in mind as well when getting a reading from a psychic. They have needs too, and health issues to keep an eye on.

If you need a past life regression, then when you have it done audio tape it so you will hear yourself from the other life. Past life can help you find out what is causing your current illness. For example, a fear that is unexplainable. Always have a past life regression done in person. Do not let anyone scam you into one on the phone.

Your Everyday Life

All of our feelings, beliefs and knowledge's are based on our internal thoughts, both conscious and subconscious. We are in control, whether we know it or not. We can be positive or negative, enthusiastic or dull, active or passive.

The biggest difference between people is their attitudes. For some, learning is enjoyable and exciting. For others, learning is drudgery. For many, learning is just okay, something required on the road to acquiring a job. The human soul is created with the innate ability to want to learn. When a person places little to no emphasis on improving their knowledge, their minds, and their bodies, they are in effect starving their souls.

Our present outlook on life is simply based on habits, built from our response of parents, friends, and society and self. This is what forms our self-image and our world-image.

This outlook is sustained by the inner conversations we constantly have with ourselves, both consciously and subconsciously. The first step in changing our outlook is to change our inner conversations.

Positive thinking means admitting into the mind thoughts, words and images that are conductive to growth, expansion and success. It is the expectation of good and favorable results. A positive mind anticipates happiness, joy, health and a successful outcome of every situation and action. Whatever the mind expects, it finds.

It is common to hear some people say: "Think positive" to someone that is feeling down and worried. Most people do not take these words seriously, as they do not know what it really means, or do not consider it as useful and effective. How many people do you know that ever stop to think what the power of positive thinking means?

When the attitude is encouraging, we consider pleasing feelings and beneficial images, and we see in our mind's eye what we really want to happen. This brings clarity to the mind, more energy and exhilaration. Our whole being transmits good will, happiness and success. Even our health is affected in an advantageous way.

Positive and negative thinking are both contagious. All of us affect, in one way or another, the people we meet. People sense our aura and are affected by our thoughts. Is it any wonder that we want to be around positive people and shun negative ones? People are more disposed to help us if we are positive. They dislike and avoid anyone broadcasting negativity.

Negative thoughts, words and attitude bring up negative and unhappy moods and actions. When the mind is negative, poisons are released into the blood, which cause more unhappiness and negativity. This is the way to failure, frustration and disappointment, and even illnesses.

Attitudes and thoughts do not change overnight. Read about this subject. Meditate about its benefits, and persuade your mind to try it. The power of the mind is a mighty power that is always shaping our lives. This shaping is usually done subconsciously, but it is possible to make the process a conscious one. Even if the idea seems strange, try it, as you have nothing to lose, but only to gain. Ignore what others might say or think about you if you change the way you think.

Always visualize only favorable and beneficial situations. Use positive words in your inner dialogues or when talking with others. Smile a little more, as this helps to think positively. Disregard any feelings of laziness or a desire to quit. If you persevere, you will transform the way your mind thinks.

Once a negative thought enters your mind, you have to be aware of it and endeavor to replace it with a constructive one. The negative thought will try again to enter your mind, and then you have to replace it again with a positive one. It is as if there are two pictures in front of you, and you choose to look at one of them and disregard the other. Persistence will eventually teach your mind to think positively and ignore negative thoughts.

In case you feel any inner resistance when replacing negative thoughts with positive ones, do not give up, but keep looking only at the beneficial, good and happy thoughts in your mind.

It does not matter what your circumstances are at the present moment. Think positively, expect only favorable results and situations, and circumstances will change accordingly. It may take some time for the changes to take place, but eventually they do.

Please remember to say CANCEL when you speak aloud verbal negative words. We all want good out of life but most do not want to work for it. You do not necessarily have to go get a masters degree or win the lottery. They are all wonderful, however verbal positive manifestation is very powerful and is right in the palm of your hands waiting to manifest what you want out of life. Just do what this book teaches you and keep in mind you need to do this 24/7... not one day a week. If you slip and say something negative, say CANCEL and it is erased from the universe immediately. When you say something negative you release the oxygen and the negativity into the universe. Therefore you will absorb it back in when you inhale the oxygen you just released. This stands to reason if you are standing next to someone you are also taking in their negative energy coming from the oxygen they released in the air. Finally, again remember to always surround yourself in white light from the Holy Spirit first thing in the morning as soon as you get out of bed.

5

MANIFESTING HEALTH

All right, you have read all of the above and you are on your way to living a full life. You know how to banish negative energy from you and you know how to keep positive energy with you. The following sections are ways that you can manifest these principles in certain distinct aspects of your life.

Health

Whether you have an acute or chronic illness or if you are looking to be healthier overall, this is the section you will want to pay particular attention to. I want you to realize that with every client I have had come to me with a health problem, the first thing I tell him or her to do is to see a doctor. The reason I do this is the deep regard I have for the healers within the medical community. For that reason, I want you, the reader, to do the same thing prior to performing any of the manifestations that I share with you in the following health chapter.

Would not your life be so much easier if you found yourself healthier and fitter than you have ever been before?

Many of my clients have thought that and that is why I am going to share with you, the secrets of manifesting a healthier you.

The first thing I am going to do is reveal to you some of my own clients' accounts of what they have done. The following client paid attention to the rules of positive manifestation and her story is much happier than the ones that did not.

*　*　*　*　*

When Felicia first came to my attention a few years ago, I was doing her reading in my home. When we began our session, she was greatly interested in finding out about her future love life, a common question for any psychic. As I was doing a reading of her my spirit guide informed me that Felicia was very sick inside. I knew enough not to dispute George, but I believe he could sense my incredulity. I believed at the time Felicia was outwardly the model of a healthy woman. When George told me that she had a lump in her breast, I was very saddened. Felicia was usually a very kind and generous woman and I always hate to see people like that struck down in the prime of their lives.

I would not tell her straight out that she had a tumor in her breast, but what I did do was suggest to her that she see a doctor immediately regarding her breast, that I saw a lump and did not like it. As a psychic I often know bad things about the future in someone's life, and as a professional I have found ways to steer them in the direction that they need to go to so they can circumvent the problem.

A few days later, she called me and told me that they had found a cancerous lump in her breast and it was malignant. It did not take my empathic skill to know that she was frightened. As I began to soothe her down and we talked, I could sense some of the strength come back into her being. As we talked, I informed her of how she could do something about what was happening to her. As I went over the rules to manifesting a healthier body, I could tell that she was getting very positive. It was not long before she started to tell me that she was not ready to cross over and she was going to beat this. From George I knew that the lump was severe and it would take a lot of treatment and even then, there was a 50/50 chance that it would not work well enough. However, I knew if she followed the doctor's orders and maintained positive manifestation, she would succeed.

She continued to come to me for readings and she would tell me how she loved her little dog, and how she was looking forward to watching him grow. When she came for a reading it was never about her health, she was convinced that her health was not going to be an issue, and all she cared about was finding her kindermate. Every time she came to see me, her attitude was positive. Repeatedly, she would tell me that she was going to beat this thing.

As the weeks and months drew on, I could tell she was physically getting weak due to her treatments and the chemotherapy. She even told me that the doctors and nurses seemed to be treating her with a futile sense of hopefulness. I could tell it had become very bleak and the doctors thought they would lose her. However, none of that deterred her from her position of optimism.

Less then six months from the time I had informed her that she should go to the doctor, she had beaten back the cancer.

Today she is still alive without any cancer problems and she is now living in a new home, with the man that she loves. Her dog is great and the three of them are very happy together.

* * * * *

Another example I would like to share with you is concerning how you look and not just how you feel. When I first told this client the ways to live a healthier life, I was surprised by how she wanted to implement it.

*   *   *   *   *

Many years ago, I met a client by the name of Ruth. Ruth was in her mid 40's and I could tell that she took care of her mind and body. She was a very beautiful woman and she obviously did what she could to take care of her looks. As we got to know each other, I told her the way that she could keep a healthy life. In the years that went by I began to notice that her skin was becoming less wrinkled and her complexion was almost radiant. Eventually I asked her what she was using to make herself look so young. To my surprise, she told me that she was not using ANYTHING. She was simply using the same principles I talked about concerning health.

She told me she would say aloud –I will never ever age; I want to keep looking good and will for the rest of my lifetime. Of course, we will all age at one point no matter how we manifest it verbally, since it is a natural process that must take place. However, without realizing it, probably because I would have thought it was excessively vain, I had helped her achieve something that she really wanted and you can too. You can still look your best by using the process I give to you in this book.

*   *   *   *   *

Before I begin with the steps needed to manifest positive health, I want to reiterate the importance of going to see your physician if you find yourself with symptoms of an illness.

Steps To A New You

The first stage is to know what you want to manifest.

Step one: Take a piece of paper and make a list of all of the health concerns you want to improve. Be very careful when you are making this list that you do not make a mistake. If you do make a mistake as far as putting something on the list you do not need, simply scratch the item off.

After you have made your list, look it over. If you accept the list, then move on to step two. If not, then do not rewrite the list as this will place your health goals back one calendar year. If you make a mistake, then you need to simply cross out the error and move on. When you are finished with the paper do not throw the paper out. Throwing out the paper will erase it from the universal energy and you will need to start all over regarding the time frame.

Step two: In the morning, after you have erased the negative energy from the night before, take out your piece of paper and start going down the list. As you read off the list, say aloud what it is you want to fix about each individual item. Then you repeat it over again and fix what you want, say it aloud verbally.

Step three: As the day progresses, if you hear something said negatively about your physical problems simply say the word "CANCEL." If for some reason you cannot say it, then mouth it. This is known as verbal organ talk. This is the best way to solve negative cellular energy. For an example; if someone you know walks up to you and says that you are not looking good you may soon find yourself feeling poorly. Manifesting is the same thing, it is important for you to know that your organs listen to what you say aloud. What you say is a direct correlation to what you are feeling. This includes saying things negatively in a joking manner. Any form of negativity can plant a seed in your subconscious.

That is why the first thing I want you to do when you hear or say something negatively, or if you feel that you are dwelling mentally on a negative, you should say aloud "CANCEL." Once again, it is much stronger if you say it aloud. We are human and we all have negative thoughts and we hear negative things. That is why it is important that when this happens we say CANCEL. When we say CANCEL, we erase the negativity from our mind cell memory and the universe, much like erasing something from a blackboard.

I once had a client that refused to implement these procedures in her everyday life.

*   *   *   *   *

Shannon was a client I had that would constantly use negative organ talk. I would always hear her talking about having an aneurysm or having someone give her a stroke. There were many times that she would complain about her relationships by saying, "that man is going to give me a stroke" or "those kids are going to give me a stroke." I would tell her, over and over, to say CANCEL when she said these things. Eventually, at one of her readings when she said that her job was going to give her a heart attack, my spirit guide told me that she had to stop saying that or she will soon have a stroke.

I realized that her negativity had gotten to the point where her cells had almost come to a breaking point. I had to get her to stop saying it and to do a cleansing. I began by asking her, how long she had been saying things like that. She replied that she had always talked about stroking out and she would say the same things concerning her job and everything else in her life. I told her to stop saying it. I reiterated how it is negativity she did not need and if she did say it always say cancel aloud after she said these things. I gave her all the ways to cleanse her body from the negativity that she had built up within her system.

Unfortunately, she did not heed my words and it was soon after that she actually had a stroke. As a psychic-clairvoyant, I always want to help the people that are my clients, but the sad truth is that people sometimes refuse to change their behavior. Whenever I see that happening, I know I have to accept that because we all have free will.

*   *   *   *   *

There is an optional step four that is for people that have a debilitating disease in the family. Who are actually suffering from such a disease or even a broken body part. For many people that have a family history of a medical problem, they will bury that fear deep within their subconscious. When that occurs, they may begin to show symptoms of the disease. This may occur even if they never mention the disease, because the fear has, in essence, done the manifesting itself.

Step four: If it is a problem concerning a broken limb, or any form of illness then you will need to do the following exercise every night before you go to sleep.

As you lay in bed, you will need to close your eyes lightly. Then you need to relax your body as much as possible, being sure to breathe in and out deeply. Surround yourself with the white light from the Holy Spirit. Imagine you are going into your nose or mouth area and being able to see inside your body, as if you are an energy or a bright light. Go right to the area that you are suffering from. Imagine you are cleansing the area or pouring liquid gold all around the problem area. As you do this, you will need to use verbal organ talk. "I am ridding my health issue and sending positive healing cells to...and name the area."

Then imagine you are bringing yourself up and exit through either the nose or mouth, I prefer the nose. This is a very easy and general exercise and highly effective.

The reason for doing this is that every cell has its own energy. With the help of positive verbal organ talk, we are able to activate the cells in a way that cannot be done without it.

George says that everyone has the ability to produce cancer cells and this is a good way to keep certain cells from ever producing them within your body. Fear of cancer or heart disease can trigger the activation of negative cells.

By following these steps, you greatly reduce your chance of having these types of problems.

Doing positive verbal organ talk will help you to be healthy, vibrant, and give you greater opportunities within your lifetime.

This is similar to visualization, but with positive verbal organ talk you talk to your organs much like you would talk to a friend. Another difference between visualization and verbal organ talk is when you visualize and believe that it will happen. Most people have a difficult time doing visualization. However, when manifesting using positive verbal organ talk, it is more effective and is easier. When you say things aloud, you are effectively telling your brain, as well as the universal energy, that it is ok to do it. When you visualize, your brain tells your body what to do. This uses the right side of your brain. On the other hand, when you verbally manifest aloud, your voice tells your brain what to do while at the same time you are activating a positive change within the universal energy and your cellular energy. Always remember to give positive feedback to the universal energy. When you do, anything is possible.

I want to talk to you about organ transplants. I am sure everyone has heard of someone that has received an organ transplant and they are known to act differently. When that organ was in the original host, it had its own cell memory. When it goes into the other body, it carries over the mind cell memory with it. What will eventually occur is that the recipient of the organ will not just have a part of another person's body part inside them, but also a part of their mind cell memory.

*   *   *   *   *

I would like to share one last interesting example. Animals are affected by positive verbal manifestation. Of course, we all know they cannot speak aloud. Nevertheless, we can do it for them. A client of mine, Jeanette, had a dog and she noticed a lump under around the breast area. She took it to the veterinarian and they told her it was cancer. Her dog was fairly old and there was not much the veterinarian could do other than cut him open and hope he lived through the procedure. She told me she would talk to the dog and rub the tumor area and say you will be ok aloud. She said she would show happiness and joy when she rubbed that tumor area. The dog picked that energy up because they do understand, even though to a lesser degree of course. However, the dog's cell mind memory kicked in and absorbed it and carried it throughout the dog's cells. The dog lived beyond the time she was supposed to. Two years beyond.

*   *   *   *   *

Manifesting Relationships

In the 38 years that I have been reading, the most asked about problem people come to me for has been about their relationships. I want to help you get the best out of your relationship. So many times I have had clients come up to me and ask me, "Celest why isn't my relationship working out," or, even, "Why is it so hard to feel good about the relationship I am in?" The stories I have given you below are just a very few of the ones that I have helped over the years. Even if you do not see your specific problem mirrored by the tales of my clients below, I can assure you that whatever the situation, the rules I ask you to apply will be able to show you how you too can find your true kindermate.

Later in this section I will show you ways that you can improve the relationship you are in now as well as solve the problems you may experience in the future.

*   *   *   *   *

Jacky was a client of mine that did not like to talk aloud to manifest the positive things in her life. She was a mature woman and wanted someone to be a companion for her. I told her to write it down on paper like I had instructed earlier in the book for positive health manifestation. I told her to read it over everyday, several times a day, the same list, on the same paper. She still did not think it would work for her, because she did not get out of the house much. I told her to stick to what she had planned for the day and keep doing this. I told her to make sure she wrote down what she really wanted. If she wanted to change her mind after she started it would take a lot longer.

She trusted me and did what I had told her she would need to do. Within a few months, she ran into a man while she was out grocery shopping. Well low and behold this man was one of her kindermates. They have been companions ever since. By sticking to her daily activity list and reading her positive manifestation list, she had met the man she wanted.

* * * * *

I met Mark about one year ago. When he came to me for a reading, I could tell that this was a man that had almost everything in his life going well. He was successful, intelligent, well fit, and generally a positive man. As we talked, I found out that he was in the process of having his house built. To him, this meant the only thing missing was a real solid relationship to build his life on.

I told Mark of the ways to manifest a positive relationship and how he could find his kindermate. After our readings he told me that the woman he was meant to be with would come into his life before he was done building his new house. Soon he was telling everyone that was close to him the same thing, his friends, neighbors, and relatives. Whenever he would talk to them they would constantly tell him that there was no way he would meet the woman of his dreams before his house was completed. I told him that he should refrain from talking about his dreams with those that are so negative unless he said, "CANCEL" after they do.

Mark came to me the day after his house was complete and told me that he had met a great woman the week before and from what you told me about recognizing a kindermate, I believe she is the one.

He got his woman several days before his house was built, and they are still together to this day.

*   *   *   *   *

Sheri was just out of a violent relationship with her spouse, when she first came to see me. I worked with her over and over to try to heal her mind cell memory. She was so negative because her ex used to tell her she was ugly and would not get anyone if she left him. The amount of negativity that her former spouse placed upon her had truly warped the way she viewed herself and the world around her.

In truth, she was beautiful inside and out. It took me a few sessions just to get her to stop telling herself that she was not useless and that she was beautiful. After I worked with her, she began speaking aloud using positive manifesting and she was saying she looked great and felt beautiful. I convinced her to go to a spa and after that, she found her true kindermate in less than four weeks.

That released her negative mind cell memories.

*   *   *   *   *

I had a client named Sarah. She was always worried about being in a crowd of pretty women and felt she wouldn't be able to find a date in a club full of pretty woman. I told her about the means of positive manifesting for a kindermate. Sarah is a pretty woman in and out, but kept saying that no man would ever pick her out in a crowd. After she used my method that was no longer the case. Soon she started to do what I told her to say and do and she *found a great man. The man was her kindermate and she had met him in a club. It was with this man that she eventually married.*

I found she did this negative talk from a past life experience or a soul cell memory.

*   *   *   *   *

I had a client named Mary; she was single, and never married. Whenever I would read her, she would always say negative things regarding men. I would always tell her during our readings that I see her kindermate coming by soon. She would say "NO Celest, I have a bad track record with men and I will not ever be happy and find my kindermate." She manifested it verbally. To this day Mary will not stop her negative talk and unfortunately, she is very unhappy.

This is an example of a negative way to manifest.

*   *   *   *   *

I cannot stress enough the need for positive verbal talk. That is the reason why there are so many divorces in the country. I cannot tell you through the book what you the reader may be having a problem with, I can only do that during a reading. However, I will share with you the reasons I have seen and I will show you some examples of what I mean and how to stop it and make your relationship positive. If you have a kindermate, there are still other reasons why you may not be having a good relationship. Therefore, what I am going to do is teach you some simple steps, to manifest a positive relationship in your life.

First, a kindermate is someone we have on our contract from the otherside. We have at least four in one lifetime on earth. We do not always meet all of our kindermates in our lifetime though. This happens for various reasons. They may live in another country and we just never cross paths is the primary reason.

We do not always contract out that we want to meet all four kindermates in our lifetime.

We have different degrees of kindermates in each lifetime. For example, I have a reading and I tell the gentleman that he has two kindermates in his life. What happens is one may be the highest level of kinermate, say one is the first –the highest kindermate and the other is the 4 the highest. There are times the fourth highest may be the best choice for us because the first highest may have mind cell memory problems or soul cell memory problems. A true psychic can tell how high a level kindermate someone is by actually seeing the kindermate cord and the color of the lining of the cord.

There is a chord that exists between kindermates. It is almost like an umbilical chord. The chord varies in size width and color depending on the closeness and level of kindermate. No one can just look at someone and tell how he or she ranks as far as importance in this life for kindermate. The physical look between two people rarely has anything to do with how high a level kindermate someone is. I know not everyone is psychic, but most people will be able to sense if someone is a kindermate.

The following exercise is what I tell people to do if they want to find out if someone is a kindermate.

Sit on a chair and clear your mind and think with your head. By that, I mean think about the person in the same way you would think about your job or the chores you have to do over the next few days. This is what I mean by thinking with your head.

Then close your eyes and picture an arrow going from your head to the middle of your chest. Focus on the arrow in your chest.

Now, think about how you feel about someone you love. This could be your best friend a parent or even a pet. Doing this will show you what you think with your heart.

Then keeping your eyes closed, I want you to see the red arrow and it should still be facing down. Next take the arrow down to your navel and stop, an inch above your navel. Then blank your mind and you should get the answer.

By doing this you should be able to know whether that person is your kindermate. I have to make you aware that once you have received your answer, do not analyze it. Do not do it again. Chances are you will get a different feeling if you try. My Spirit Guide tells me what happens is that your subconscious kicks in and you alter the feeling to suit what you want and not what is.

The next thing I am going to talk about is soulmates. This is the one thing that I have a problem with. Soulmates are not kindermates. Soulmates are on the otherside. You cannot meet a soulmate on this side. If you go to a psychic and she or he tells you that someone is a soulmate then they are lying at best or frauds at worse. Soulmates are on the otherside and they are dead. By that I mean they have no physical form. They are not a part of the living. A soulmate is someone you have been with in this lifetime on earth and they have passed away or crossed-over to the otherside. When you both reunite, that is your soulmate.

Kindermates are on this side as a living breathing person. We have Kindermates on Earth when we die, and we may meet up with them on the otherside. My Spirit Guide tells me that there is a forty percent chance that we will not meet them. The reason for that is this, they are being reincarnated back to this side. Now, if they are someone that is the highest kindermate that you have and they crossover now ahead or behind you, there is a good chance you will see them on the otherside.

Manifest a Positive Relationship

The first thing I want you to do is to make a list of the top ten most important things to you in a mate. Do not make it more than ten and if you want you can make it less. Once you have it written down, keep the list. Do not throw it away. When you make a list, if it something you want then make sure you keep it. If you throw the list out then what you are doing is throwing it out of the universe. If you do that then you will have to do it over again, and you will be starting from step one. I like to place it in my calendar. The reason I put it in my calendar is that it almost gives the energy of the universe a timeline with which to accomplish a task. You can manifest anything you want if you do it properly and if you are sure within yourself. There is also a little saying that I believe is important to remember when you are making out a list or asking to manifest something in your life, "Be careful of what you wish, for you may surely get it!"

If you go to a fake psychic they may say to you that you are going to meet someone that is 6' 2", 210 lbs, with hazel eyes, and a crooked grin. Well you may go home and think about this person, and then you will tell your friends and co-workers. You will be thinking about it a lot for instance, as you walk through the mall, if you are at a restaurant, or even just walking down the street.

What happens is that even though that psychic was fake you have so much energy out there to meet this man that it may actually come true. Unfortunately, it does not mean that this person is your Kindermate. It could be this is the worst person for you to be with. Your mind is so powerful that it can manifest almost anything.

The steps are simple for calling forth a positive relationship.

Step One: Before doing any manifesting, it is important to bring the white light around you and say aloud, "God please protect me from any negative relationship energy."

Step Two: State aloud and clearly that you are looking for your kindermate. Do not say that you are looking for your highest kindermate, just say kindermate.

You want to do this on a daily basis first thing in the morning when you wake up.

Step Three: Create the list that I had discussed earlier. Always remember to make your list only ten items long or less. With that in mind, it is important that you stress the things that are most important to you. Do not make the list too complicating. The following list is an example of what you might fantasize about, but it might be the wrong thing to write out:

6' 0"
180 lbs.
Blonde hair down to just above his shoulders.
Perfect teeth.
Strong jaw.
Blue eyes.
Fit.
Well endowed.
Smart.
Sophisticated.

The reason that you might not want this person is because you almost described Ted Bundy the serial killer, one of the personifications of a dark entity. With a list that is no longer than ten items, it is important to really think about what you want in a general sense, like this:

Handsome.
Healthy.
Great smile.
Gentle with a strong sense of self.
I.Q. between 110 and 145.
Has a dry sense of humor.
Enjoys romantic getaways.
Loves rock music.
Creative lover.
Likes to dance.

With the above list, you can add certain things like instead of just handsome you may want someone that is also African-American, Nordic, ect. The key is to make sure the things that are most important to you are in the list. Then go about your daily routine. Throughout the day, you may see someone or meet someone that has a physical aspect that you would like to have in a mate or a personality trait, which you are looking for. Such as a co-worker with great eyes, or a friend that has a sense of music. Then say it aloud to whomever you are with or say it to yourself privately. Do not get too specific, like the fake psychic earlier.

A kindermate is someone that is connected to your inner self. If you ask for a kindermate with a lot of specific physical characteristics then there may not be anyone out there like that, but if you just choose general things like; race, tall, short, thin or thick, then it becomes so much easier for you to get your kindermate. If someone is with you and he or she is not someone you can talk to about your Kindermate, such as a boss or something, then say it mentally or go to the rest room and say it aloud. I do want to remind you that if you do it mentally it is not as effective as verbal so you should remember that feature in your mind and when you have the time speak it aloud.

Fixing the Problem

Kelly, a client, once asked me why her and her mate had such divergent sex drives. She would tell me that he seemed to want intimacy so much more often than she did. From my readings, I knew that they were high-level kindermates. The everyday problems that are in every couple's relationships can damage even a relationship between two high level Kindermates. Remember, we may be with a Kindermate, but we still have to work on our relationships. This is very important. After we discussed the problem, I told her the best way to handle the situation. Through the positive manifestation, they have made their relationship stronger and more vibrant.

* * * * *

I had a client come to me named Marcy and she was

confused about her relationship. She told me that her mate and her got along so well it almost seemed like a fairy tale. However, it came out that she was miserable in her fairy tale life. This can happen due to sexual incompatibility. If they are kindermates, this can be fixed.

*   *   *   *   *

I recently had a client come to me for a reading and she asked me what to do when you love your mate and he is a high kindermate, but his genital area is too small. If you are with a high kindermate and you get along so well, please remember we are looking at the soul and if you say negative things regarding the size of the genital area, you are manifesting yourself to tear down your perfect Kindermate. You are programming your mind cell memory to shut that part of your relationship off. Sure, you can get a mate that is better endowed; however, they will not be a Kindermate. If the size or look of someone is the most important thing then you are not looking for a true kindermate.

*   *   *   *   *

I had a client named Richard that complained about his

wife's refusal to perform certain things in their bedroom.

*   *   *   *   *

Janine came to me complaining that her husband did not perform long enough to satisfy her.

*   *   *   *   *

John wanted his girlfriend to get certain body parts enlarged, but she was unwilling.

*   *   *   *   *

Every one of the above problems can be solved either through proper communication, acceptance of your partner, and/or positive manifestation.

I have probably done approximately 450,000 plus readings of various types over the years. Through them, all the most demanding of subjects seems to be about Kindermates. Everyone seems to have an opinion concerning the person we are with or not with at the time. Having a high-level Kindermate is not always going to be the answer to happiness. By the time we have joined with a mate, life itself has already put its prints on the person we are with. If they have chosen a certain life that you cannot at present accept, then there will be problems within the relationship. If your kindermate has for one reason or another been tainted to becoming a dark entity, then it is more important that you be safe away from your Kindermate. However, usually the things that keep us from being happily involved with our kindermates are others, sex, and finances. All three of these things are fixable.

In many situations, it may seem that the people around us are more knowledgeable about our relationships then we are, or at least that is the way they would like us to think. Many people like to tell others what to do in regards to your relationship problems. Like he or she is not good for you, you are wasting your time with that person, and if they were meant to be the one, it would be easy. Unless the Kindermate you are with is causing you pain, then the truth is, it is not a relationship that you should throw away so easily. If it does not happen right away you may give up. That does not mean it is not suppose to happen, just that the timing is off, the middle journey sometimes takes time. Do not listen to what others have to say. Feel it in your gut and go with your heart. That is why the divorce rate is high, we give up too fast and pick the wrong ones that are easy and end up trying to win back the Kindermate even years later.

When we are on the otherside and want to be

reincarnated over to try it again, we arrange it with a soulmate on the otherside. Remember, a soulmate is one that is dead and is on the otherside. We arrange to come back and try it again in a new lifetime. So, therefore they are meant to be. However, we can have a one level Kindermate on earth and they are not as compatible as a two level Kindermate on earth. Just because we have a high one level Kindermate, they may have soul cell memory baggage, chemical imbalances or even mind cell memory baggage, and you would be better off with a second level kindermate as I mentioned earlier in this book.

Everyone has a different sexual drive. What you need to do is to write down what you feel is the weak points in intimacy. Realize that everyone is going to have his or her own list.

If you do not think you are a good lover or you have a spouse that is incapable of sustaining their own pleasure for you to achieve satisfaction, then you will use two things to achieve the goal you want. First, communicate with your spouse. Let them know of the problem. Many times, this is something they do not even know is a problem. Then you will use the power of the mind using positive verbal communication. If it is a man that needs to slow down his excitement, or a woman that has problems reaching satisfaction, either way it can be achieved through this method.

Concerning the list you made, you will notice on the top ten was the mention of a creative lover. This does not mean for a one-night stand. However, you will want to add in certain general things that you want from a lover. For example, a lover that takes charge, a compassionate lover, someone that likes to experiment, also things for high sex drive or low. Do not include things like I want him very well endowed or for men I want a woman that is top heavy. These are physical traits. So unless these things are the key to your happiness and you cannot enjoy a relationship without them, then do not write them down.

Concerning any current relationship you may have, what you should do is think about the problem with the relationship and really think about what is the cause of the problem. Your lists should include things that you need to work on, as well as things they should work on.

When you talk to your lover, tell them one at a time what it is that needs to be tweaked. Then the two of you should write it down on a piece of paper and go to your quiet spot and say aloud, "I will no longer fear or have a problem. I will move forward." Do this on a daily basis. Your mind will let you know when you are ready to move on.

Another area of the relationship is financial security.

George tells me, do not base your relationship solely on financial security. Also, remember you are not building a Ken doll or a Barbie doll, so keep that in mind when you are asking for relationship things.

Look at it like this. The economy is not the best, so there are many people that are walking around without a lot of cash or great expensive suits. You should take a sheet of paper and write on one side what you have as far as financial, this should include job, property, cars etc. Then on the otherside, write down what you would like to improve. Let us say you make $25,000 and you would like to improve it to $65,000 and you have an apartment but you would like a small house in the suburbs. Well the difference between the two is what you should want from a mate. Go down your list and see the comparison. On the other hand, if you find someone that is higher than that level, then that is great. Although, you need to be realistic in what you ask for. I have found over the years that financial security is a tricky subject when it comes to readings. Always remember to use positive verbal talk when discussing anything in your life, relationships, jobs, money, and even friends.

You can manifest good and then manifest bad and ruin the good.

Positive Personal Finances

I had many clients who never went to college and they are now making more money than those who did. They spoke aloud and manifested it. They would say aloud how they were going to get a job that pays a 6-figure income a year, and would say it over and over and over. They would write it down and do everything I wrote for you to do in this book. I read them now and they are making big money. What you ask for, is what you get back.

*   *   *   *   *

I had a client who needed a job desperately. They told me they went on interviews and would tell the people interviewing them, this will work well with my husband's schedule or my children's schedule, or even when do I start? They got so many job offers it was unreal.

*   *   *   *   *

A bad example of the above would be my client Teri. She would go on interviews and talk to herself in her car on the way down to the interview, I am never going to get this job. Well how do you expect to get it if you cut the process in pieces? She even left town and still had trouble getting a job.

* * * * *

One of my clients would call the person who interviewed them on the next day and ask them what their schedule would be when they start. So many people are afraid to do this they feel it is not professional and desperate. That is not so. If you want something, go and get it.

* * * * *

Some of my clients would place an ad in the local paper and cut the ad out and put it on the refrigerator. Every time they would walk past it, they would say aloud, "I will get a job before the ad runs out of days." They usually got one before the ad was taken out of the paper. This is a form of writing it down and saying it aloud, with of course a cleansed and healthy cell mind memory.

* * * * *

I have endlessly helped so many lately with this economy being so bad the past few years. If you want a job, you will get a job. It all depends on how much positive manifesting you say aloud. This is where people are stuck. They see the economy is bad and when they apply for several jobs, they end up giving up fast. However, the truth is, this has become the normal period to get hired for these jobs.

*   *   *   *   *

I recently had a client, Peter, look for a job and after he learned the exercises to manifest a good job I gave him, he launched one right away. He would get ready for an interview and say I got it, and wouldn't tell anyone in his family or his friends he was going for an interview, because they would end up saying you wont get it...too many people are out of work and you stand no chance. Stay away from negative verbal comments. When he did the positive manifesting, he got a job right away.

*   *   *   *   *

I had a client named Ellen. She had trouble finding a good friend that would not betray her. I told her to never pick a friend who is always saying negative things. If they do it all the time it will go onto you, and like I explained earlier; that will stick to your mind cell memory and cause you to create negative things from life.

* * * * *

I had a client, James, who was a healer and always had negative friends constantly drilling his mind with problems. He was always trying to fight against them and trying to fix his life up because he was picking up the negative verbal talk and it was going on to him. When I told him to move on you do not need that, he did and is very happy in his life now. I am not being mean telling him that, however, we do not want this to affect our life and usually they wont stop having problems and running to you. Take care of your mind cell memory and soul cell memory.

* * * * *

I had a client recently tell me, "Celest, my friend is flirting with my boyfriend." This is not a friend to be around. Trust me, do not waste time with a friend like that. Too many people keep saying they are human and make mistakes; yes, they are human and make mistakes but why let it mess your life up. Do not let them just move on.

* * * * *

I recently told a client, Sue, "If your friend is not happy for you when you have something to rejoice over, then they are not a friend to be around. They are negative and this will cause you too have negative energy in your life." Please stay away from those kinds of so-called friends.

* * * * *

So many clients want to own their own house and not rent. I had a client who did not have any money and could not get a loan. She drove up and down the streets looking at places to buy. However, she knew she did not have any money and could not get a loan. She ended up getting involved in a lawsuit with her ex husband and she got the dream house she picked out. She kept saying, "I will get a beautiful house."

* * * * *

I had a client make a list of what he wanted, car and home included. He read the list aloud daily and kept reading his list from the same paper he kept in his calendar like I instructed in this book. He did this for about a year and got his car and house. He wanted to pay it off right away. He did He ended up landing a good paying job and bought his car and paid it off the day he bought it. He met a friend who built homes and he built him a home at a very good price.

*   *   *   *   *

My client Anne had a nice house; she told me she used to look across the street when she was sitting on her porch and admire her neighbor's house. She said to me she would say aloud on her porch," I would love to buy that house soon." She used to say it over and over and look at this house as she said it. She said it from her heart and not just the words. Two years later, her neighbors moved and she got the house she thought she would never get because her neighbors had no intentions of moving.

6

IRAQ

There are so many clients asking me if I would touch base on the spiritual side of Iraq. With all the sadness and with so many lives being taken, I would like to first express my condolences to the victims and family members of this war along with all the men and woman who are serving our country, and also, all the men and women that have served our country in the past. I greatly respect and honor you!!

I will only touch on subjects regarding what is happening in the spiritual world in Iraq, and what happens to those who crossover so suddenly and to those who are evil.

First of all, we do not write on our contract we would like to be involved in a war and be harmed or killed. This is the middle of our journey and we can cross paths with Evil and darkness. The middle of our journey is huge and a lot can take place. I call it the snags or bumps in the road. However, George my Spirit Guide, tells me those who are involved in a war or an awful tragedy like 9-11, are at a very high level. High level meaning they are spiritual learners and are special souls.

We must honor them and pray. Prayer is huge and if everyone prays together, you send this message out to the universe. You release it. Remember, say it aloud like I mentioned in this book. Verbal positive manifestation is extremely powerful.

Well your probably asking, "Celest, there are so many of us praying all over the universe now regarding the pain over in Iraq, why isn't it working?" My answer is if, no one was praying and sending positive verbal talk out to the universe, it would be much worse. The prayer is helping!

What is going on over Iraq is the middle and working to the outcome.

Soldiers Who Are Killed

Again I would like to express my deepest sympathy to the family and loved ones of these special souls who were killed.

These men and woman did not chart they would crossover by fighting a war. Again they are special men and woman at higher levels, but they did not chart it on the otherside before they carnated over to this side.

My Spirit Guide George tells me when a soldier is killed very fast, they are taken over to the otherside immediately by their Spirit Guides. This is why we all have Spirit Guides. They guide and help us in times of need. Many clients ask me, "Celest, what happens if they die fast?

Are they earthbound?" The answer is NO. They are high level souls and their Spirit Guides are all around them and their guide will take them over to the otherside. At times, when a person passes quickly they do not know they are dead, they feel disoriented. This did not happen to our soldiers over in Iraq.

Here is what happens. Say they are killed very quickly, their Spirit Guide is at their side and takes them very swiftly to the otherside. They are a little disoriented from their soul making a fast exit, however, Spirit Guides are on the otherside to nurture them back. They wrap them in warm blankets and explain what has happened. Spirit Guides will do this for as long as it shall take until their soul is adjusted to what has happened. They are well taken care of. The hardest part is the family and loved ones who are on this side, who suffer the a loss of a loved one.

What You Need To Do

If you are someone that has lost a loved one over in Iraq, you need to speak aloud and talk to them. They hear you. Everyone who passed can hear when you are speaking to them. If you did not get to tell them what you wanted when they were here on earth prior to their death, talk to them now and tell them. Tell them how you feel or any unfinished business you needed to share with them. You can light a candle (I prefer white) and speak aloud to them. Pray aloud, and if you wish, keep talking to them when you feel you need to tell them something. They need to see they are not forgotten. Please do not forget to speak aloud. This will help you and they will know that you are aware they are in a good place.

Captured By Terrorists

First, I would like to explain to you the reader that I understand these are very sensitive topics, but George wanted me to talk about them since I get so many clients asking about these topics and they are in panic thinking the worst. Remember, we are all carnated over as pure souls. It is the middle the learning, that can make us dark only if we choose to become dark.

When a hostage is captured by a terrorist, we all get so frightened by this horrible evil person capturing a pure soul. It is very traumatic to the one being held hostage and to family members, loved ones and to the public.

Please know these hostages did not write in their contract on the otherside they wanted to experience this. They happened to get in the path of a very evil person.

They did not do anything wrong at all, they just happened to be in the sight of this very dark, evil soul.

It has nothing to do with anything the hostage ever had done in the past or present. I want to make this very clear. I am going to explain what happens during this time to the hostages. Your are probably asking me, "How do you know this Celest?" Well, my Spirit Guide George tells me and I can get into the minds of the captured and feel them as an Empath.

When someone is being held hostage and is being prepared to crossover by the evil terrorist as in the beheadings, those being held captive tend to feel less and less fear. God makes it this way. When the evil terrorists' are harming the victims, please know they do not feel the pain you think they do. Let me explain, God takes that away from them. If you have ever spoke to an abused man or woman they would also tell you when they were being beat up and left for dead, they felt a very spiritual healing and surprising enough, they did not feel the pain that was being put out to them. God, Angels and Spirit Guides are wonderful. I am not God of course, but I am positively sure the information I gave you is correct. When they are murdered, they are swiftly taken over to the otherside and cared for by Spirit Guides. They are also wrapped in warm blankets and nurtured until they feel they are adjusted.

What I mean by adjusted…when you come back from vacation you think what do I do first; laundry, sleep, or prepare for work. They would feel the same for a very short time.

What You Need To Do If A Loved One Being Held Hostage Is Murdered

What do you need to do if our loved one is captured? First pray aloud. Think positive and tell God aloud you need strength from him. Speak aloud to your Spirit Guides and Angels, asking them to give you strength. Say aloud, "I call at least 12 Angels to watch over me and give me strength." Light a holy candle or if you do not have one, light a white candle as white is pure. Then speak aloud to your loved one who has been murdered. Tell them you love them and that it was ok to go, even though they will be terribly missed. Tell them aloud how proud you are of them and that you understand they crossed paths with an evil soul by accident. If you have anything they owned, such as a pin or a chain, wear it. They can see this and will know you are comforted by this. Remember, on the otherside they are not sad and do not feel pain. Here on Earth we do, and you need to let the otherside know you are ok. Tell them of any unfinished business or thoughts you need to share with them from this side to the otherside.

Only do the above as much as you can handle. You do not have to do it if you wish not too. Everyone heals and feels pain in different degrees than others. Do not force yourself.

In my chapters prior to this one I mentioned that if someone murders another, they will need to carnate over right away if they know they did wrong. Please let me explain. A soldier that has to kill for his country will NOT be carnated over right away. They are doing good and the world needs discipline or there would be a lot of chaos in this world. Can you imagine a world without discipline? A soldier enlisted to help their country. They are special souls and they are very much needed. What would we do without these courageous men and woman?

Suicide Bombers

Suicide bombers are a crafty, evil soul. A soul who turned on the dark side. Again, and as I stressed above, we are all carnated over with a clean fresh start a pure soul. Just like erasing the blackboard we now have a fresh start because this is why we wanted to carnate over. Not to buy more clothes or watch more soap operas or maybe get a new car. We take the missing, learning section of our recent past life and we come back to better it...to pass our lesson finally.

The suicide bombers did not write in their contract that they would come back as a suicide bomber. We are all pure on the right side of the otherside. They took evil a step forward over and over again, completely opposite of what they wrote in their contract. Just as the terrorist did, they are all associated with evil.

We all can turn our life around even if we are on the wrong path of darkness. However, terrorists choose to feed from this dark side and grow darker. We do not have to be labeled a terrorist or suicide bomber to go under this category. Anyone who becomes dark stands the same reason. When these suicide bombers cross over, their souls will indeed have to carnate over IMMEDIATELY to do this all over again. They have no choice but to do it again.

A woman or a child who <u>had</u> to have strapped a bomb onto their clothing is a different story. They did not want to do it and had no choice in the matter. They also know right from wrong. They will not have to carnate over immediately in this case even if they caused so many deaths and injuries. They knew it was wrong, but was in the hands of evil and had no other choice. When the victims are killed in this man-made horribly evil attack, their Spirit Guide will take them over to the otherside swiftly. This is what Spirit Guides do. They are with us everyday and guide us. In circumstances like this one, their Spirit Guide is by their side and will immediately send them to the light of God on the otherside.

Please be reminded that we all carnate over as pure souls. With all the horrific tragedies taking place over in Iraq, every one has Angels and Spirit Guides beside them to watch over them. Even the evil have their Spirit Guide to watch over them. The Guides are very disappointed, but they do not leave their side. Spirit Guides feel there can always be a chance the evil can try to turn it around. Spirit Guides are assigned to us from the beginning and will remain by our sides no matter what, until the very end. There are situations when someone is dark and they hate to leave after they cross. They are a lost soul as this is where ghosts come into play. There are times those brave men and woman who fight for our country come face to face with evil or on the grounds of darkness. They are most certainly looked after by there Spirit Guides and Angels. Always put white light from the Holy Spirit around you to protect you from negative energy when you feel you are in the circle of darkness.

Please Remember

These men and woman who fight for our country are not being punished for anything they have done in the past. I have found they are the souls of a high level. They are of Angelic energy. Does it not make sense why we have such pure souls fighting for our country? I would sure hate to see dark evil fighting for our country.

Why Don't Spirit Guides Help Save Their Lives

Spirit Guides in the course of a day send us so many messages. They give us signs. One of them is a gut feeling. Even a psychic cannot read themselves. Throughout the day you may see numbers that maybe match someone's birthday or license plate number. Or you may hear names of the one you need to focus on. You may turn on the TV or radio and hear the name of a loved one you are worried about. This is a validation your Spirit Guides are sending out to you. It is their way of saying, "It is OK to draw attention to that person." You can keep much safer if you listen to these signs.

How To Listen To Signs

1. Sit in a quiet room and clear your mind, even a minute is appropriate.

2. Learn how to identify the present existing things around you. Take only one day at a time. Do not look back on yesterdays events.

3. Focus on things that have taken place today, start from the time you get up in the morning. See what you have accomplished.

4. Now the rest is easy. Just live life one day at a time and learn to identify with things around you. For example, did you see anybody that looked like the loved one, friend or pet you are worried about. Did you hear any names around you of that person. Also maybe you saw someone in the store that looked like this person you are concerned about. In numbers, you may see plate numbers of someone's birth date or their favorite numbers thrown out to you.

Always speak aloud positive verbal communication for the loved ones we have over in Iraq. Even if you do not know of anyone who is actively involved in the war still say aloud *–I place the white light from the holy spirit to protect the men and woman over in Iraq to keep them safe and to return home safely.*

Below is something you can do from the time you get up in the morning to the time you go to bed to send positive energy by using positive verbally words.

1. After you awake in the morning, say, "God protect me with the white light from the holy spirit to prevent me from giving and receiving negative energy." I gave this prayer to you earlier in the book. Say this first three times then right afterwards say, "I also place the white light from the holy spirit to protect and guide those men and woman over in Iraq, our soldiers. Keep them safe until then return home."

2. Then say, "I call at least 9-12 Angels for each man and woman over in Iraq to protect them. To be by their side from the time they get up until their day is completed." Then ask for another set of Angels to watch over them from the time they sleep until the time they awake. You are sending Angels around

the clock to watch over them. When you ask for an Angel, they will come!

3. Think of them at least once a day and say aloud, "Stay strong dear men and woman who are fighting over in Iraq. You will be coming back safe and sound."

If everyone does this daily we are sending them Angelic healings and sending their way positive verbally manifestation. And what possibly can be stronger than that.

If You Returned From Iraq

If you are one that returned from fighting in Iraq you need to think positive and say aloud positive verbal talk. Imagine your soul that is in the middle of your chest, in between your breast. It did not write what you went through in its contract and your soul needs nurtured just like you do. The mind is separate from the soul. The soul wrote the contract and is saying to your mind, "Come on I want my outcome to happen. I'm ready."

Remember, you did not write this on your contract and you did not do anything to deserve what you witnessed or were forced to do. You are a special soul and we honor you!! You need to verbally aloud say good things about yourself. Say aloud, "I am honoring myself for what I set to accomplish." Stay only around positive people so your soul can heal faster. Bear in mind you have been though a tremendous amount of stress.

When you go to bed at night say aloud verbally, "God please erase any negative mind cell memory from all I experienced over in Iraq." Mind cell memory is what your mind in times of trauma never forgets. You can erase this by saying that. Say it every night for a few months or as long as you need too. Talk to those who have passed on, maybe someone you have witnessed passing, maybe it was a friend. Talk aloud to them and tell them what you wanted to say to them and never did, or tell them how you are feeling in regards to their crossing. Be very detailed when you are doing so.

All of the above will help you heal, nurture and manifest positive energy to manifest a positive outcome, the outcome you wrote on your contract.

I am so very proud of everyone over in Iraq. Those fighting, and the ones we lost who have crossed-over the otherside. I take a bow to you all with the highest respect.

May God continue to Bless each and everyone of you.

7

WHAT SHOULD YOU BE SAYING

Be courageous. Change and improve each day. Do your best and do not look back. See learning and change as opportunities. Try new things. Consider several options. Meet new people. Ask many questions. Keep track of your mental and physical health. Be optimistic.

Make a positive commitment to yourself, to learning, work, family, friends, nature, and other worthwhile causes. Praise yourself and others. Dream of success. Be enthusiastic.

Keep your mind focused on important things. Set goals and priorities for what you think and do. Develop a strategy for dealing with problems. Learn to relax. Enjoy successes. Be honest with yourself. Manifest daily and with a positive attitude.

Studies show that people with these characteristics are winners in good times and survivors in hard times.

7 Suggestions for Building Positive Attitudes
· In every day, look for positive people to associate with.
· In every conversation, look for one more interesting idea.

- In every chapter, find one more concept important to you.
- With every friend, explain a new idea you have just learned.
- With every teacher, ask a question.
- With yourself, keep a list of your goals, positive thoughts and actions.
- Remember, you are what you think, and you feel what you want.

Positive thinking means admitting into the mind thoughts, words and images that are conductive to growth, expansion and success. It is the expectation of good and favorable results. A positive mind anticipates happiness, joy, health and a successful outcome of every situation and action. Whatever the mind expects, it finds.

Not everyone accepts or believes in positive manifestation. Some may consider the subject as just nonsense, and others scoff at people who believe and accept it. It is quite common to hear people say: "Think positive!" to someone who feels down and worried. Most people do not take these words seriously, as they do not know what it really means, or do not consider it as useful and effective. How many people do you know that ever stop to think what the power of a positive cell memory really means?

Positive cell memory and negative cell memory are both contagious. All of us affect, in one way or another, the people we meet. This happens instinctively and on a subconscious level, through thoughts and feelings transference and through body language. People sense our aura and are affected by our thoughts. Is it any wonder that we want to be around positive persons and shun negative ones? People are more disposed to help us if we are positive. They dislike and avoid anyone broadcasting negativity.

Negative thoughts, words and attitude bring up negative and unhappy moods and actions. When the mind is negative, poisons are released into the blood, which cause more unhappiness and negativity. This is the way to failure, frustration and disappointment.

In order to turn the mind toward the positive, knowledge and training are necessary. Attitude and thoughts do not change overnight.

Read about this subject. Meditate about its benefits, and persuade your mind to try it. The power of thought is a mighty power that is always shaping our lives. This shaping is usually done subconsciously, but it is possible to make the process a conscious one. Even if the idea seems strange, try it, as you have nothing to lose, but only to gain. Ignore what others might say or think about you if you change the way you think.

Always manifest only favorable and beneficial situations. Use positive words in your inner dialogues or when talking with others. Smile a little more, as this helps to think positively. Disregard any feelings of laziness or a desire to quit. If you persevere, you will transform the way your mind thinks.

Once a negative thought enters your mind, you have to be aware of it and endeavor to replace it with a constructive one. The negative thought will try again to enter your mind, and then you have to replace it again with a positive one. It is as if there are two pictures in front of you, and you choose to look at one of them and disregard the other. Persistence will eventually teach your mind to think positively and ignore negative thoughts. In case you feel any inner resistance when replacing negative thoughts with positive ones, do not give up, use the white light and place this around your body if you need to. Keep looking only at the beneficial, good and happy thoughts in your mind.

It does not matter what your circumstances are at the present moment. Think, and talk positively. Expect only favorable results and situations, and circumstances will change accordingly. It may take some time for the changes to take place, but eventually they do.

From the beginning of the Old Testament to the ending

of the New Testament, words were spoken by God, Jesus, the disciples and things happened. The Bible shows us by example that words play a very large part in our life. Thinking and speaking positively is something that will bring about healing, prosperity, joy and love.

Speaking and thinking righteously will bring about great changes in your life if you will speak with confidence, believing that what you say will happen because it is the will of God! Phrase it like this: I am a new creation; I am a brand new person. Old things are passed away, I am born again.

Words can bless a speaker or they can curse a speaker. Words will heal or make you sick. How you speak about yourself and others has a direct bearing on what the mind creates. Words that ridicule, torment, harass and tear down a person will never bring life. Thoughts that are always fearful and bitter will never remove fear and worry. We have what we have because we speak into existence.

When we constantly tell ourselves or our loved ones that they are no good, or that they are stupid, we instill the words into their cells and it becomes reality to them and to us. Phrases like the following will lift the heart and mind and restore life: "My words work for me. I fill them with a power that cannot be resisted. I fill my words with faith and love. My words bless. My words heal. My words lead my loved ones into victory. My words charge the atmosphere of my home with faith and love. I am a winner."

What we say and think makes a difference in our life. Our words are the keys to abundant life. Unlock the door to your life of abundance by keeping a watch on what you say and think.

Your life is a series of stories and you are the author.

Read the sentence again. Did you realize this? Does it scare you or make you feel powerful?

If you think about it, it is a very cool thing! Moreover, it goes way beyond the glass half empty ~ glass half-full concept.

Positive verbal manifestation can bring inner peace, improved relationships, better health and success. The daily affairs move more smoothly, life brightens up and there is more happiness and satisfaction.

Positive thinking is contagious. People around you pick up your mental moods and are affected accordingly. Think about happiness, good health and success and you will cause people to like you and desire to help you, because they enjoy the vibrations that a positive mind emits.
Effective positive manifestation that brings results is much more than repeating a few words or telling yourself that everything is going to be all right, and then letting fears and lack of belief enter your mind. Some effort and inner work

are necessary. Are you willing to make a real inner change in you? Are you willing to change the way you think? Are you willing to have a vigorous mind that can influence your environment, and the people around you?

Always use only positive words in your inner dialogues. Use words such as, I can, I am able, it is possible, it can be done, etc.

Accompany your inner dialogues with feelings of happiness, strength and success.

Do not heed negative thoughts.

In your conversations with other people, use words that evoke scenes of strength, happiness and success within their minds. By doing this you will want to associate yourself with people who think positively.

Think positive, manifest positively and you will find that the world around you will begin to be positive to you.

Always be willing to fill your mind with light, happiness, hope, feelings of security and strength. At worse, you will be a happier and better person.

Understanding the inner powers, developing, strengthening and using them will make a great change in your life. When the mind concentrates on one single thought it becomes powerful and can achieve wonders. This action is similar to a magnifying glass that concentrates the rays of the sun into one single beam, and projects it on a piece of paper, causing it to burn.

Do not be afraid to succeed. Fear is the manifest killer. You can succeed. You will succeed. You have already started to succeed.

www.ingramcontent.com/pod-product-compliance
Lightning Source LLC
Chambersburg PA
CBHW030935090426
42737CB00007B/441